WAGER THE WILD LAND

A Paraplegic's
Triumph Over Tragedy

David E. Harper

Wasteland Press

www.wastelandpress.net
Shelbyville, KY USA

Wager The Wild Land:
A Paraplegic's Triumph over Tragedy
by David E. Harper

First Printing – February 2012
ISBN: 978-1-60047-682-2
Front cover portrait photo by Matt Daniels

Printed in the U.S.A.

0   1   2   3   4   5   6

To my wife, children, and
To all those tormented
By difficulties in life, and
To my God who I hope has ultimately
Been glorified by my life

Awareness of danger is not likely to deflect the course of mankind, for man does not live by bread alone. "All man wants," wrote Dostoevsky, "is an absolutely free choice, however dear that freedom might cost him and wherever it may lead him." True enough, most men run almost mechanically like clocks from their birth to their death, motivated by their biological needs of the moment and by the desire to feel socially secure. But their very passivity makes them of little importance for social evolution. The aspect of human nature which is significant because unique is that certain men have goals that transcend biological purpose.

Among other living things, it is man's dignity to value certain ideals above comfort, and even above life. ...As long as mankind is made up of independent individuals with free will, there cannot be any status quo. Men will develop new urges, and these will give rise to new problems, which will require ever new solutions. Human life implies adventure, and there is no adventure without struggles and dangers.

-René Dubos. *Mirage of Health: Utopia, Progress and Biological Change.* New York: Harper & Row 1957, 277-278.

ACKNOWLEDGMENTS

I am deeply indebted to many people who have been involved in the development of this book. First, I thank my best friend, my bride who stayed by my side and has loved me throughout the years, although at times I didn't deserve her love. Many of these adventures would not have occurred without her beside me. She encouraged me while I wrote this book, even though she battled for her life during part of its preparation.

To all who reviewed this, I offer my humble thanks. Your help and interest kept me pressing forward. My heartfelt thanks go to my father and mother for the perseverance and faith they instilled in me. Although my mother passed away before I wrote this, my father provided deep insight in its preparation. He encouraged me toward publication with the words: *a faint heart never won a fair maiden.*

Many times I voiced the urge to quit working on this project. I'm grateful to everyone who encouraged me to stay the course. This book is in your hands because they believed this story needed to be told.

Many thanks go to Marcia Hornok for getting me started down the path of publishing and for editing the manuscript before it was split into two books. Susan Giffin provided outstanding editorial and formatting skills during the final stages, steering this work to its publishing goal. Thank you for your careful editing and personal interest in this book – including the title.

Foremost, I thank God my Father in heaven, who pursued me throughout the course of my lifetime. Even when I wanted nothing to do with Him, He saw purpose and meaning in me. His longsuffering and loving kindness extends to all. This I hope to share with you the reader. I have prayed often for you that God will use this book in your life in a special way. May you discover God's extraordinary strength, as you wager against your own struggles in life.

TABLE OF CONTENTS

CHAPTER ONE

Untamed Point of View

Crow hopping and spinning out of control like a red tornado, the horse I was riding careened over the desert, hurling me from the saddle. As I headed for the ground, thoughts of my wheelchair back at the ranch corrals flashed across my mind. *Would this hurt as bad as some of the wild wrecks that that hurricane deck has given me?* Today, I can say that being caught in a trajectory between the immensities of heaven and earth, unable to use my legs, is one of those rare occasions in life, as the saying goes, that conspicuously separates an incident I'll always remember from one that I'll never forget.

This wasn't the first time I found myself airborne, however. Nearly eighteen years before this event, I broke my back in an auto accident while returning home from a weeklong trip in the mountains. The car in which I was riding swerved over the edge of a snowy precipice into a rocky chasm hundreds of feet below. During the split seconds of weightlessness while the car plunged into the void, I prepared to be snuffed out like a bug. Staring out the windshield at the looming chasm racing toward me, I was sure there was no earthly chance of surviving. Miraculously though, my time to die had not arrived.

Afterward, not content to live the quiet life of an invalid, I persisted in the rigorous outdoors lifestyle I loved. Exploring different ways to expand access into rugged country, not conducive to a wheelchair,

1

became a way of life. Adding to a long list of experiences, I began pushing my limits by riding saddle horses three years earlier. Now, deep in the heart of Oregon's cattle country, I was about to discover the outer boundaries of my limits.

Spring weather sent winter into full retreat when my wife, two children, and I arrived at the ranch in Shumway, Oregon, where my brother Jerry and his wife Nancy were living. We had driven from Colorado to spend Easter with them. It was spring break of 1986, and I had just applied for a field job in Wyoming. Anticipating there might be some work helping Jerry move cattle, I had brought my saddle with me. My guess was correct. A day or so later, Jerry and I left the ranch to push a few cows into another pasture. It was cool and cloudy as we rode east. Pausing to open a gate, we continued on toward a low drainage where we picked up a small herd of cattle, moving them across an open bog.

The wind picked up some, and we could feel a squall building off in the distance. Gilbert, the horse Jerry had given me to ride, was a working animal but hadn't been ridden much that winter. He immediately sensed there was something very unusual about how I sat in the saddle. Being barn spoiled during the winter, he really didn't want to be out working on this blustery spring day, and he kept trying to ease back to the ranch. Without the use of my legs to spur him along, I was having difficulty working him with only the reins. Realizing I lacked the strength of my legs, he started misbehaving. One of the real frustrations of being a paraplegic is in knowing what I should be able to do and being unable to complete the task. Sensing that I was losing control, I made the mistake of overestimating my actual ability and underestimating Gilbert.

Approaching the bog, Jerry, who was slightly ahead of me, began pushing the cattle across it toward the hill on the other side. On the edge of the bog, Gilbert balked at crossing it altogether. He had had enough. The horse wanted to return to the corrals. I moved him toward the left and hoped he'd follow at Jerry's crossing. By then, however, he had made up his mind and turned toward the ranch.

Gilbert was a good horse and would have crossed under the encouragement of any other rider who could physically take control of him. He had my number, though, and had figured that I lacked the power to turn him. Becoming annoyed at my own inadequacy, I thought I might bluff him and smartly pulled the reins to correct his retreat. He seized the challenge. Twisting sharply to the left, he bucked his hind legs to the right while whirling like a cyclone in a tight circle.

In moments, it was all over. My right foot flew out of the stirrup. My useless left leg just crumpled under me, unable to use its stirrup to pull him around. To add insult to injury, Gilbert then moved into the bog to unload me. Too late, I grabbed for the saddle horn and wound up with a handful of muck. Down in the mud, all I could see were four hooves dancing about in what I rashly wanted to believe was an effort not to step on me. Reduced to a clumsy ballet between hooves and elbows, I fought to roll clear of being trampled. It was one of many times over the past forty years I've wished I could use my legs.

Jerry turned on the hill opposite the bog to see my rodeo unfold and watch me roll to a standstill. Exasperated, I threw the handful of muck back into the bog and spit some dirt from between my teeth. The water seeped into my clothes, as I pulled myself up onto drier ground. Jerry came trotting over, rounding up Gilbert. "Are you all right?" he said.

"Yeah, I think so," I said sheepishly, conscious of the fact that I'd just been unceremoniously dumped off my horse. Inventorying my limbs to make sure they all bent the way they were supposed to, I added a bit of light heartedness to assure him. "I just thought I'd dismount right here and rest for a minute."

Jerry helped me back up on the horse and, after a few words with Gilbert, we continued moving the cattle. Later that day back at the ranch, I discovered a few bruised places I was too proud to make public. Lying low for a few days, the soreness worked out slowly. This incident illustrates my determination to enjoy the rugged life I love, even if it throws me for a loop.

The stage for the drama of my life's story stretches from the cold northlands of Alaska to the arid Mojave-Sonora deserts in the South. From the rugged Pacific Northwest coast, it ascends to the grand heights of the Rocky Mountains and beyond. The props include horses, four-wheel-drive pickup trucks, snow machines, ATVs, canoes, motorboats, helicopters, and small fixed-winged aircraft. Oh, yes, I almost forgot: wheelchairs. Furthermore, the people in these landscapes have been an integral part of my success. Thus, much of my story has taken place in remote rural areas.

It could be said that for the past four decades, I have been gliding through life in a wheelchair. Surely it's true that I move without placing a foot on the ground. On the other hand, the rural lands have been everything *except* smooth. Many of those places lacked paved roads (sometimes even lacking roads), let alone sidewalks. It's been my destiny to discover that wheelchairs don't function well in quicksand and that they can provide a thrilling ride a mile down a mountain face.

Other times, I have learned they inconveniently break in the backcountry, where, of course, there is an absence of parts stores; some strange ingenuity must be applied to limp my chair back to civilization. My skills have been tested by the need to sidestep my wheelchair in the path of a runaway horse. Another time, an aggressive goshawk's violent air strike challenged my agility to hastily evacuate its territory.

Before I go much further I need to clarify something for the reader. Since I don't walk, I've never quite known how to convey the idea of moving from one place to another. 'I wheeled down the path' sounds awkward and doesn't really fit, since *I* don't wheel—the *chair* does. Where others may say 'I took a stroll,' 'I took a wheel' seems to escape the point and might be interpreted by some that I went on a binge. Actually I take all four wheels wherever I go even though they're not always in contact with the earth at the same time, but whatever. What's more, in some of the stories I tell, 'I careened down the path' may actually be more true to the point. I've told people that I've ambulated or perhaps perambulated, and I've received a blank stare. So I usually just say, 'I took a walk,' and leave it to my listener to decide if I walked pushing my chair or *pushed my chair as I walked.*

We may be faced with the best and the worst situations in life simultaneously. Life may bring terrible predicaments, like being bucked off a horse. If we live through one of life's wild rides, we can brag about it later. At the time, there certainly is nothing about which to brag. Sometimes we must tie a knot in the end of our rope and hang onto it! When the ride explodes, there isn't time to organize our finest moves or plan a graceful dismount. We're in the saddle; now deal with it. Get tough! In the colloquialism of the Old West, horsemen referred to the saddle on the back of a bucking horse as the *hurricane deck.* That's how I've come to regard my wheelchair.

Comparing my ride in a wheelchair to riding a bucking horse is a bit over the top. Folks true to the saddle might take offence. However, my chair has given me some unexpected rides that feel like a hurricane blowing beneath me. During those times I've been compelled to say to myself, *Hold on, feller; if it doesn't knock you senseless, it'll probably be okay!* This in fact describes my life.

Rural America, from its tundra, mountains, valleys, plains and fascinating people, is an awesome landscape with legendary character. For me, living in this setting, even though confined to a wheelchair, is a privilege that I've never taken for granted. The legend of this landscape is part of my day-to-day life. Those in urban America might doubt its existence.

My daughter and her husband moved to Louisiana a few years back. Pointing to a picture of the Grand Teton Mountains near Jackson Hole, she told her boss. "I was raised near those mountains." Her boss told her that she was full of nonsense; such a place couldn't really exist. But places of such grandeur do exist. The landscape influences the men and women who have spent their lives in the shadow of mountains such as these. I cannot overstate how the rural West has affected my life perspective from a wheelchair.

Remote rural landscapes tend to give the local people a colorful quality, matching the rugged character of the land. One person may have dirt on his boots, calloused hands, and a PhD. Another may have a high school education and yet be a county commissioner with statewide notoriety because of his business savvy. Women drive cattle on the open range, operate heavy equipment, build houses, and forge political destinies. It's not viewed as competing with men, but simply doing a job. Together men and women fight fires, conduct search and rescue, and take charge of social events. They are a mixed complexity of hardy, polished, poised, rugged, temperate individuals. This is the normal culture.

Of all their characteristics, though, one of the remarkable qualities among those people that I know and respect is that they don't whine or complain much. I have a good friend who rode fifteen miles out of the wilderness with a broken pelvis after his horse exploded into a rodeo over rough ground. He wrapped his belt around his hips, cinching it down tightly to draw his pelvis back into place, and then rode out on his own strength. Although in excruciating pain, he gritted his teeth and accepted that it had to be done.

I have departed from this taciturn tendency to speak of my pain and struggles in this book only to the extent necessary to connect with others who endure suffering. I hope my story might encourage others to overcome their own difficulties. If I were to dwell on my weaknesses, struggles, and hardships, I would never run out of things to write about, and the reader—and I—would eventually become bored. Rather, I have mostly chosen to dwell on the many enterprising, adventurous times in my life. I occasionally remind the reader that my struggles are constant; they are very real, and I must overcome them on a daily basis. This is how I live my life.

The larger-than-life country surrounding me overshadows my paraplegic condition when I work alone in remote areas. The demanding land extracts a heavy toll for a simple mistake such as forgetting a coat on a sunny day. In the past few days as I've written in this book, the weather has gone from 70° down into the 20s with deep snow over the region. As I went out before daylight to go hunting this morning, I saw that the temperature registered -1° last night. It may become colder before it warms up again. During the twenty-seven years that I've lived in the Rocky Mountains, I've witnessed similar conditions during every month of the year. Out here, the land demands that a person live by all of his or her wit and potential. There may be no one to rush to rescue the unprepared. My aching back or my friend's broken pelvis pales in light of what else might happen. Certainly, the harsh and exacting land, with its rugged people, has imbued itself on my character.

Being confined to a wheelchair is a tremendous inconvenience, yet hard-wired in my soul was the deep desire to take the roads less traveled throughout rural America. I have no regrets for choosing that route. It has not been an easy one to follow, but it has given me great satisfaction because of the wonderful people who have also helped shape my view of life. What I have to share here may be alien to some, but the message of living to the fullest potential, I believe, is applicable to everyone.

In these rugged settings, I have enjoyed being able to push my limits beyond the confines of my wheelchair. This is a special blessing and privilege. It is true that I have often overestimated my ability, landing me in some precarious situations. I have discovered time and again that 'stupid' hurts in many shapes and sizes, yet this is all part of the adventure that I have yearned to live. The folks here spurred me on to a greater life than I would have encountered otherwise. Moreover, they have helped me to attempt challenges I would have only dreamed of facing. When I am old and worn out, I hope I'm not sitting in a rocking chair, wishing I had made more effort to do the things I had dreamed of doing with my life.

It's not all challenges; there is a witty side of my life also. Playing into the forces defining my life are the euphuisms and antics of folks in the rural West. These may seem peculiar to urbanites. A person suddenly startled might have a 'deer in the headlights look.' Someone confused might look like 'a cow staring at a new gate.' A guy or gal who's gloomy or angry may be 'wearing a thundercloud.' Someone sad, 'wearing a rain cloud.' A person who's unfriendly may be said to 'have the personality of a crowbar in January.' We might say that a guy who's stretching his story to a breaking point is 'telling a windy western.' Someone not accomplishing much is 'eating soup with a fork.' When a person needs to stop whining, they'll be told to 'cowboy up.' When they complain too much: 'they're bawling like a calf.' A stupid mistake can make a man 'as nervous as a long-tailed cat in a room full of rocking chairs.' If a person's struggles are more than she can bear it might be said, 'she's got a hard row to hoe.' Water is about 'as scarce as a sheepherder in a cowboy convention.'

Animals like the jack-o-lope exist only to tease the naive, and snow snakes somehow evade even a chance sighting. Finally, folks will let you know that snipes can only be hunted at night. These are additionally part of the complex synergy that forms my attitude toward my condition.

Sometimes I have been compelled to respond to events in a puzzling or even comical way. Those who are innocent to my perspective on life and unaware of my capabilities may find that things are not what they expect of a guy in a wheelchair. This leaves them open to my mischief. Most of the time, I try to be sensitive toward the mindset of strangers. On the other hand, poking a little fun at someone else's expense can be inevitable. A prank or practical joke, spontaneously erupting in the hardest part of a job, has brought the entire operation to a standstill. This habit is not always appreciated by the slaves of urban industry, but offers a break to the often rigorous, unique life I lead. The object of such comical relief may be anyone.

Once, my wife Barbi and I moved onto a remote rural homestead, which had not yet caught up with such modern conveniences as electricity. Furthermore, the nearest telephone was over a mountain at the end of the county road two miles away from where our rough access road began. There it sat in its own glory, a proper urban telephone booth in eloquent loneliness. It was a real novelty because the nearest town was twelve miles down country. The well supplying water to our house had an old Aermotor pump jack driven by a Briggs and Stratton five horse-powered gasoline engine.

Barbi and I were busy working at the wellhead one day, completely focused on what we were doing. It had been tough work, and we'd been at it for a couple of hours. Suddenly I sat straight up and cocked my head toward the house.

Inquisitively she asked, "What's the matter?"

"The phone's ringing!" I burst out sharply. "Quick, grab it!" Of course she could cover the distance uphill faster than I could. She crossed a full fifty feet at a dead run toward the house before she pulled up short, realizing she'd been duped. There was no phone.

I too have been the brunt of an occasional practical joke. Once, in California, a fellow killed a big rattlesnake and cut off its head. I was busy clearing brush, completely oblivious to what he was doing. Mischief filled his heart, and he couldn't wait to share this little snake-killing episode with someone, and I was the only one around. He sneaked up alongside me and tossed this snake onto the ground at my feet.

Surprised by its sudden appearance, I instantly attempted to evacuate that piece of snake-infested real estate under my chair. Spinning my wheels in reverse, the dirt turned into an instant dust storm, as the dead snake's reflexes caused it to writhe before me. I nearly worked myself into a full-blown panic before I realized its head was missing. The prankster later said that he considered tossing it across my lap, but decided if it caused me to miraculously rise and walk, he was afraid I might have hurt him.

Another time, I was in the timber, cutting firewood in Wyoming with Bill, an amiable big-boned guy a few years older. He was a forester by profession and in his element. We had selected an area choked full of wind-fallen trees that looked like a giant's pickup sticks. Inserting earplugs, I grabbed my saw and went to work on one edge of the trees, and he set out for the other. I had worked my way into a tight spot that didn't give me much room to negotiate. Littering my retreat route with sixteen-inch long blocks of firewood, I managed to trap myself in the downed trees. With a wide-brimmed hat pulled over my forehead, I was chain sawing logs right and left in a hurry to get home. Sawdust was flying everywhere. Bill had worked toward me into this thick mat of timber and was within forty feet of my position. I was only vaguely aware of his exact location.

As my chainsaw wound down after making a cut through a log, I suddenly heard, "Timber!" Tipping my hat up slightly, I glanced around to see where his tree was falling. From beneath my hat brim I saw the lower part of an enormous tree coming right at me. Terrified, I dropped my chainsaw. My escape was blocked! Preparing to jump from my wheelchair under the nearest deadfall, I jerked my head up to focus above the brim of my hat. (Bill later told me I turned white.) This expanded perspective allowed me to focus on the upper reach of the tree. To my relief, about twenty-five feet up the trunk, the treetop had snapped off like a matchstick during a previous windstorm. Bill, being a forester, had gauged where the end of the tree would land and knew it would fall short of hitting me.

My eyes fixed on its ragged end just before I bailed out of my chair. Hitting the maze of windfall logs surrounding me, it made an awful sound, but it was barely audibly over the sound of my heart frantically pounding out an SOS behind my earplugs. The ragged edge was pointing toward me at eye level ten feet away. Bill was at the butt end, holding his saw in one hand, belly with the other, and roaring with laughter.

At times there has also been a bit of recklessness in my insouciant attitude toward life. Once, while climbing a hill on a snow machine at full throttle, I plowed through a snow cornice at the top. Suddenly my sled and I were airborne. My legs flew out from under me and for a few split seconds, the only part of me connected to the snow machine was my death grip on the handlebars. The rest of me flew in the breeze like a distress pennant from a ship's mast. Landing at full throttle, the snow machine plowed into the powdered snow below, creating a blizzard in which, my friends later told me, I nearly disappeared from sight. My stomach knotted with the fear that if I let go of the snow machine, the deep snow just might conceal my body until melt-off in the spring. Giving it full acceleration, I powered out of the hole, with enough momentum to propel the sled across the surface. I rose up enough to see ahead; my belly rested on the seat with my legs dragging through the snow when I came to a halt. My friends were watching in disbelief. Of course, I acted as though it was true grit that kept me going, but the back of my throat had sure gone dry.

This type of excitement has been the story of my life. I believe a man is created to live a life of adventure, no matter his condition. It is for each of us to decide where and how that can be accomplished. To be an adventure, there has to be a challenge beyond the familiar that is not altogether predictable. The less predictable the challenge, the greater the adventure. Unpredictability makes challenges compelling. Yes, we must calculate our risk, so that we don't seriously hurt ourselves or others. Not everyone can blow through a snow cornice! Our adventures are our own, just like the stories we have to tell. We can reach for the potential God has given us. Mark Twain once said,

> *"Twenty years from now you will be more disappointed by the things that you didn't do than by the ones you did do. So throw off the bowlines. Sail away from the safe harbor. Catch the trade winds in your sails. Explore. Dream. Discover."*

Then again from an early age, I have never been a stranger to confrontation with unexpected situations.

CHAPTER TWO

Constrained by Circumstances

As a youngster, I was drawn to places of remote solitude. My Dad spent long periods teaching me woods lore, instilling confidence in me. With each new journey into the forest, traces of the city were swept away from me. I came to love the loneliness I experienced outdoors. At times when predicaments caused me to tumble, Dad encouraged me to get up, brush myself off, and go on with what I was doing. This encouragement eventually became a maxim inculcated in my mind. Over time, he taught me how to survive with the meager resources at hand. Starting at the age of three, I learned to shoot a rifle, handle a bow and arrow, build a fire, and other skills to meet the unexpected in the wild back country.

Dad always kept a six-pound, double-bit axe in his pickup truck. Standing the handle upright on the ground, the axe was nearly as tall as I. To me it was enormous. When I was eight, he taught me to cut firewood with this axe. "When you get older, always carry an axe in the woods with you," Dad would say. "The wind might blow a tree down across the road blocking your way home. You can always cut through it with an axe." Dad taught me there were many ways an axe was useful. This simple item could provide shelter, fire, and food for those who knew how to handle it. A person needed only to observe his surroundings to discover what might be available.

Being independent-minded, I absorbed these lessons, quickly learning to survive with whatever resources I found at hand. By the time I was five, I was carrying a .22 Cal. rifle during our journeys in the woods. As I grew, I spent days hunting and wandering alone, as much from habit as from choice. I felt comfortable being alone. It expanded my confidence to cope with whatever came my way. The liberty of an open sky overhead and unfettered horizons brought complete satisfaction. While roaming the woods of the Pacific Northwest, I developed a strong sense of self-reliance.

Inspired by the wonders I observed in the mountains, I drew pictures of scenic landscapes when I was kept inside. Art released my soul from the confines of walls to the freedom I craved. The pictures I drew reflected my distaste for indoors, and the outdoors set me free. Consequently, my early pictures were devoid of people and human trappings. Stirred by the freedom I found in the open air, I truly desired to work an outdoors occupation one day. Mentally, I took home the details of each trip I took in the wilderness. I traced those special places from memory on scraps of paper with pen or pencil. Along the lonely margins of civilization, I gathered the strength and energy to break away from domestic restraints and to set my eyes on distant horizons.

Before I turned five, Dad began to teach me how to paddle a canoe. As I grew, I found myself quite comfortable canoeing in most situations. By the time I was twelve, I had spent days and nights on the rivers or marshy flood plains with a friend. We often looked for sea-bound ships navigating the lower Willamette River. Spotting a ship coming our way, we would race the canoe into the river to ride the wakes cast off the ship's bow. Other times we'd glide out to uninhabited islands in the Columbia River to hunt. Often we'd end the day lying on the warm sandy river beaches, watching the clouds roll to regions beyond our horizon. While the sun sank in the western sky, the balmy river breeze blew its course downstream. We'd let the river and the world slip by us like a dream, imagining the far-off lands we'd one day visit.

When I was in the fifth grade, our class studied the forty-ninth state of the Union. We studied how modern pioneers had harkened to the voice of its nameless valleys and unclimbed mountains. Through years of toil and strife, they settled her borderlands and sought her riches, yet hundreds of thousands of acres of land remained unclaimed. It beckoned all who were brave and hearty enough to endure her hardships. Robert Service wrote of the northland:

> *"This is the law of the Yukon,*
> *And ever she makes it plain;*
> *Send not your foolish and feeble;*
> *Send me your strong and your sane;*
> *Send me the best of your breeding,*
> *Lend me your chosen ones;*
> *Them I will take to my bosom,*
> *Them I will call my sons…"*

To me, Alaska became a land mystique, with phenomena such as the taiga at the edge of the boreal forest, the mysterious northern lights, and the midnight sun. Also there were the barrens and the bush where a man could walk a thousand miles and never cross a road. It was possible to disappear forever by simply walking off the pavement. It was the 'great alone.' As I grew up, Alaska was a place that constantly haunted my subliminal thoughts.

My friends and I yearned to live in Alaska. In the misty shadows of the river bottom on cold and cloudy days, we would huddle around a smudgy campfire in a dingy clearing framed by the tangle of broken hardwood forests. Wrecked and ragged, these woodlands possessed the haunted remnants from the occasional purging of the mighty Willamette and Columbia Rivers. In the circling smoke that burned our eyes, we'd discuss Alaska's mysteries in low voices, while rain faintly tapped against the ground. Secretly I'd wonder if I had the mettle to be her chosen one. Sizzling on the fire would be the small game we killed for the lunch we forgot to pack. Even then, we needed nothing to survive but the woodland tools we carried.

One time, a friend Marty and I bolted for the woods on a soggy day to escape household chores. He was a big-boned, red-headed kid a year older than I and quiet by nature. Mom had pulled the vacuum cleaner out of hiding, which was always a sign to any red-blooded American boy to find something to do quickly.

On our flight into the hinterlands, his two brothers, Randy and Mike, begged to go along. As we trudged off down our escape trail, it began raining, and before long we were all as soggy as the forest around us – and hungry. We were two miles from home, but going back meant being confined indoors to clean house. Marty had the insight to stuff a pack of crackers in a haversack, as he slung it over his shoulder heading out the door. But crackers were slim rations.

We built a fire and began to warm up, just as a pigeon landed under a nearby railroad trestle. Mike, perhaps six or eight years old, said, "I'm so hungry I could eat that bird!" In an instant, Randy hurled a rock at the bird and broke its wing, sending it careening to the ground. We were on it like a pack of wolves. None of us had ever cleaned a bird, but we all knew what a dressed chicken looked like. With pocketknives flashing, we went to work. In no time, bird feathers were everywhere and the bird was on a spit across the fire. Crackers and pigeon made suitable rations for the day. With the hunger pangs at bay, we pushed deeper into the marshy woodlands and didn't arrive home until suppertime.

About the time I turned twelve, I began working during the winter months with Dad in a garment factory after school and on weekends. At first it was general maintenance, painting, and minor building. Later the job focused on preparing woolen material for shipment, renovations, and electrical rewiring. I never thought too much about it at the time, although it was hard work.

During my fourteenth year, I had a 440-volt electrical plug and outlet blow up in my hands, vaporizing the metal and severely injuring me with second and third degree burns. The wounds took weeks to heal. I took it all in stride, although the bandages frustrated my quest for adventure. I knew I was destined to become a man one day, and the more prepared I became, the better chances I would have for success. The electrical explosion became part of my training toward that eventuality. I remember how satisfying it was when I reached the age of fifteen and received a raise to $1.45 an hour.

As I grew older, comfort with the sights and sounds of the night skies and endless horizons became fixed in my soul, far outweighing urban security. During the winters in my early high school years, I ran a trap line in addition to my factory job. Often I left school in the middle of the day to check my traps. My head dazed from all the nearness and incessant chatter of students and faculty; I simply needed to be away from the swirling masses of humanity. I would throw my coat over my shoulder and start walking.

On a cold January day when I was perhaps fourteen, the evening darkness overtook Marty and me earlier than we expected. We had a choice of coming out the long way after dark or swimming a slack water. We both inclined toward few words, so it took no time to reach a decision. Stripping down to the least amount of clothing, we slipped down to the water's edge. Breaking through the shore ice extending six or eight feet out we began swimming, keeping our stuff dry on top of our heads. Needless to say, the experience was breathtaking. Arriving on the opposite shore, we quickly dressed and built a fire to warm ourselves before we headed home.

I was absent so much from school my sophomore year that I hardly recognized my classmates. Caring little for the people around me, I rarely spoke to anyone. I didn't have a single friend in my sophomore class. Sick from a head cold, I went to school on a miserably cold and stormy day in mid-winter only because it was warm inside. As usual, I didn't take note of anyone in the classroom except the teacher. Stuffiness in my head combined with a fever and chills left me lightheaded. The warmth inside the classroom instantly seduced me. I felt like melting into the chair. My eyes were burning and heavy, so I closed them for what I thought was a minute and put my head down on my desk. Suddenly I jerked my head up scanning the room. Everybody in the class looked different, and I felt disoriented. I tried to listen to what the teacher was saying but nothing he said made sense to me. The only clock was in the hall, and I felt so unsettled that I brazenly slipped out of my chair and through the classroom door. As soon as it shut behind me, the entire room erupted into laughter. The hall clock told me my scheduled class had long since passed. Apparently my class had left, and a new one came in while I slept, and I was none the wiser. Being a loner, the only lesson I learned was to avoid school even more, *especially* when I was sick.

In the summer, I worked six days a week as a field boss in a farm labor job to earn a little income for school clothes and other needs. The wage was only $1.00 an hour, but I made up for the lost income by working longer hours. Besides, I much rather preferred to work outside. What little spare time I found on those warm sunny days I spent in the mountains.

During a summer weekend when I was perhaps fourteen years old, my dad and I were on a high mountain lake, fishing and enjoying the day together. We were watching some men move erratically in a boat nearby, when they suddenly capsized it. No one wore a PFD (personal flotation device.) Dad and I had seen it coming and instantly went into action. At the scene, we realized we could not haul them on board without capsizing our own craft.

"You two young fellows stay here and hold onto the bottom of your boat!" Dad barked. The older gentlemen were showing signs of hypothermia. "Grab hold of the gunnels of our boat," Dad commanded. "We'll relay you to shore first." When we neared the shore, I jumped from the boat and helped the two in the water to dry ground.

Later, Dad told me he was amazed, as he headed out into the lake to get the younger guys. "When I turned to look back, David, I could see a strong curl of smoke in the treetops. It was impressive how fast you got a fire going!"

I swelled with pride knowing I had met with his approval. The guys later sent us a letter of appreciation, thanking us for saving their lives.

While rough outdoor living underscored my life, it was more than just being outside. In my veins pulsed the music and mysteries of the great unknown. My head throbbed with a desire to know wisdom greater than anything man had to offer. I believed I would one day discover such wisdom in the natural world. Others accepted the fact that their thoughts became inured with radios, dances, cars, and sports. Still others were satisfied with the gentle salve of religion. In my heart, I knew there was something deep and mysterious that was being obfuscated by all the civilized dissonance. Surely, the path to wisdom lay in the ways of the wilderness, and I wanted desperately to find it.

Canoeing the rivers and backwaters near my home, running my trap line, hiking, hunting or fishing took me away from the cacophony of domestic life; they brought me immense satisfaction. However, after spending a week with a sixteen-year-old friend, Red Williams, camping and canoeing on a high mountain lake, an event changed my life's course forever—shattering all my dreams. This incident altered my life in such a dramatic way that later, my life before it seemed like a distant dream.

On June 28, 1968, Red and I were returning home early in the evening and encountered an early summer snowstorm. In the back seat were Red's two stepbrothers, five and six years old. Red's stepfather was driving the car. Unfamiliar with summer snow conditions, he lost control of the car sliding in the snow toward the edge of the road. I was sleeping comfortably, exhausted, as the car began to slide. The erratic movement and a horrendous scraping sound, as the car careened along the edge of the road, instantly jolted me awake.

My eyes focused, as the car abruptly plunged into thin air. At that moment, I had no fear. As a teenager, I viewed life as either black or white. Whether life worked for or against me was of no real consequence; the only thing that mattered was the adventure. My life had seemed like a shooting star stretching from a tail of insignificance to a bright ball moving through time for no particular purpose other than to serve me. I felt it would ultimately end in a radiant fizzle absorbed in vacuous darkness. Going over the edge of the precipice, I faced certain death, viewing the plunge as merely a violent, wild ride that would end my life in the eternal abyss. I had turned sixteen years old the month before.

The impact on the rocks slashed metal and shattered glass, as launched objects ricocheted throughout the vehicle. The car crashed and rolled repeatedly against the jagged rocks below, spewing glass and rocks into my face, slamming me from side to side into one thing and then another. Helplessly I clung to the vehicle before crashing through the side window. The vehicle came to rest far beneath the highway. Then everything went black.

Later, dazed awareness drew my mind to something moving across my face. It was a dream-like sense. A mixture of rain and snow softly landed on my face, while something warm and sticky ran down my cheek past my ear. Red seemed to be levitated, drifting over me moving his hands across my eyes. I could feel him fussing with my face, and I wondered how he seemed to be able to float. My ears were full of debris. The whole world was silently rotating in slow motion. For a moment, it was as if I was a silent observer slowly turning around the scene of my own misfortune. Forty feet from the car, in the bottom of a deep ravine, my body lay crushed, a gruesome heap of flesh and bones, critically injured. I could feel a dull ache in my useless left arm. It lay limp by my side, as though it had fallen asleep and become numb; I couldn't move it. My chest felt like I was under a two-ton rock, and I thought I was being smothered.

Lifting my right arm, I tried to roll to my left and push Red aside. Abruptly the world stopped rotating. The sound of rain pounding the rocks suddenly amplified around me. Simultaneously an intense electric pain shot through my whole body, bone grinding against bone. Instantly I snapped into a world of horrific agony and freezing cold. As everything around me went black, I could faintly hear Red's voice. "Your face is bleeding, and you're hurt bad, man! Don't move! I need to…" His voice faded, as he spoke and I drifted into oblivion. Red was in mild shock, but he stuck with me.

The weather turned chilling cold with snow falling thick on the ground around me. Wearing only a Levi jacket over my summer clothing, I was slipping into severe shock. But again I regained consciousness. This time it was not with the soft detached sensation I experienced before. Throbbing pain pulsed through every inch of my body, and the slightest movement seemed to inflict a horrific amount of misery. I was draped between two large rocks, lying partially in water between them. With consciousness, I felt bitter cold seep through my clothing. Uncontrollable shaking seized my whole frame, raising me to a completely new level of tormenting agony. I tried with all my strength to force myself to stop shaking and ease the pain just a little. I hoped I'd die and was afraid that I wouldn't. Then blackness still as death flooded over me again, as the muffled sound of Red's voice faded from my ears.

I became vaguely aware that I was vigorously gnashing my teeth, as the memory that I was actually alive and in excruciating pain again brought my senses back to searing consciousness. I prayed for death or the escape of that numbing darkness that had overtaken me earlier, but couldn't force either upon myself. Hoping my life had ended when everything went black, regaining consciousness was a brutal awakening. I found myself very alive and completely helpless to save myself.

Horrendous, intense pain raced through my body. I couldn't move my legs or lift off the rocks that bound me like a magnet to their tortured jabs. They possessed the chill of tombstones, somehow portending a cryptic significance that the gates to hell were close at hand. The trees in demented mockery seemed to hurl curses at my mangled flesh. The sticky sweet taste of blood oozed into the corner of my mouth. I felt my face. It felt like running my fingers through hamburger. My fingers pushed my left eyebrow back on my forehead exposing bone.

Red anxiously brushed my hand aside. "Leave that alone! Your face is badly torn open from your forehead to your mouth, and I'm trying to fix it."

It was a living nightmare. As I lay there hour after hour in abject misery, the freezing weather added a new searing chill, as I again shook violently, slipping deeper into shock. Red had been running relays between the car and me. On one of the return trips, he carried some blankets to protect me from the ravaging storm. Most of the cold seemed to be radiating from the rocks and water beneath me. Involuntarily I continued grinding my teeth while my life drained away.

For distraction, Red told me the car lay off in the distance and that he had had to move carefully across man-size boulders to where I lay crumpled in the rocks. His two stepbrothers were still in the car. They were trapped by the terrain of boulders. Although they were unhurt, they screamed in the fear that engulfed them. Amazingly, they had ridden the car to the bottom and survived without any broken bones or serious injuries. Each time Red left them to tend to me, they screamed in even greater terror, begging and pleading with him to stay with them.

Outside of being badly bruised, all Red had to show from the crash was a small cut on his little finger. He encouraged me not to move and kept pushing my hand away from exploring my wounded face. With the passing hours, there was little more to talk about. From then on, I seemed to remain conscious.

Darkness was moving into the canyon, bringing an early close to the day. The storm clouds were thick, blocking out the sunlight. In a state of shock, I yelled for help and then tried to force myself into oblivion. After a long silence, I strained to get Red's attention. "Is there any chance of help?" I heaved in despair.

"I don't know," he answered above the din of the wind. "I can't see anything through this storm." More time passed. Red periodically disappeared to tend to his stepbrothers, leaving me alone.

At one point, he tried to climb out of the canyon, but only slipped on the rocks. During his absence, I felt abandoned. The enormous pain I suffered seemed to rob me of sleep. Blood continued to ooze from my face, caking my hair and clothing despite the snow and rain. Blood trickled into in my left eye, burning horribly and blinding me. Lying on my back and facing the sky, I found it difficult to open my good eye, as the snow mixed with rain. Swelling began to interfere with my vision. Cocooned in darkness, I fleetingly thought I was going completely blind.

Occasionally, I spit pieces of what felt like gravel and then tried to capture some of the water falling from the sky into my parched mouth. Grinding my teeth, I had sheared off all my bottom front teeth; this was the "gravel" I kept spitting from my mouth. My upper teeth were pushed out preventing me from closing my mouth.

Remembering the sound of the car grinding on gravel and the shattering of glass and metal tortured my thoughts. Then, on one of his return visits, Red yelled into the wind, "I think I heard voices up the mountain!"

Dulled from shock, I hoarsely groaned, "What'd . . . they . . . say?" My strength was waning, and my mouth was so dry I could hardly speak. I had been forced to concentrate on every word, and I wasn't really sure if I had spoken the words or just thought them. All I wanted to do was sleep—or better yet—die.

Red ostensibly replied from the far end of a tunnel. "I couldn't tell. I'm not even sure they were voices."

My head swayed, then pitched lightly against the rough surface of the rock again jabbing my face and jerking me from the sleep I longed for. Water had long since soaked through my blankets into my clothing, and the cold continued to send me into intermittent shivering.

Snow continued to accumulate on the rock-strewn bottom and mountain looming over us. As darkness fell, Red's journeys back and forth to the car took longer. In a delirious state, tortured by my own body, I finally wondered if I had been left to die in order to save the kids.

I held no real firm religious convictions when this accident occurred. I spent many years listening to messages of salvation, but I stubbornly resisted God's calling. There was no problem I could not face alone. My belief then was that real men did not succumb to religion or help. God, I believed, was a crutch for the weak-hearted. I had no regard for God or man taking what I could from life and giving nothing in return. Lying in that canyon among the rocks and desperate with fear, I craved anything that would liberate me from my misery. I cried out to God for help.

I waited. I've withstood the furious blast of many storms since that fateful day in June of 1968, but none have been as cold or as terrifying. The wild wind mocked my plea; its fury tormented the treetops until their moaning cry harmonized with mine against the rock walls. When only the wind answered in reply, I cursed God, hoping if there was such a being, I could anger Him enough to strike me dead. I didn't even know if a god was really there to hear me. The daylight hours had waned like my anguished voice vanishing in the wind. A lacy curtain of snow spun around me as darkness engulfed me.

Thus began a night of unmeasured terror and agony. To cry out for relief in the grip of death and believe that there is no greater power that can help is a most dreadful thing to experience. It hurled me into an abyss of despair, as the gates of hell gaped wide to receive its own. Little did I know then that God heard and was helping me in my darkest hour.

What I have learned through the years since then is this: God's power and His character are not constrained by human circumstances. God allows us to experience problems for our sake; to bring us into His strength when our power utterly fails us.

To say this event caused the worst pain and terror I have ever experienced in my life understates what I suffered. The pain was so intense that I fell headlong into its whirling vortex. I continued crying into the howling abyss for unconsciousness that would release me from the terrifying sirens of hell's open mouth and the excruciating pain of consciousness.

Later we learned that a traveler passing down the mountain road on a motorcycle noticed the skid marks in the snow. He stopped and hollered into the dark empty void below.

Red's stepfather had jumped out just before the car was hurled over the edge. Landing on a ledge fifteen feet below, he crippled his leg. He was trapped there. Above the din of the wind, his faint cry for help alerted the traveler that someone needed to be rescued. Unable to descend the precipice, he immediately left for help. There were no cell phones in those days. Minutes stretched into hours that tumbled into a black hole lost in eternity before help arrived.

More time passed as our rescuers struggled down the face of the icy escarpment in wind and snow, searching for a route to reach and extract us. When the rescuers finally reached us, I was so relieved to be lifted off those boulders and placed into a stretcher that I passed out in the luxury of soft, clean, dry sheets.

Immobilized from head to foot, they lifted me vertically from ledge to ledge out of that chasm in total darkness. Several times, the EMTs challenged me to live, despite my desire to die. On one particularly challenging rock face, someone holding the rope above me slipped, jolting the rope taut while I dangled vertically. All the while the canyon seemed to howl in menacing outrage at being deprived of its corpse. In the ambulance, I asked an EMT to call my parents.

Late in the evening, I finally felt the warmth of a hospital. My parents were waiting there, but they were told that I probably wouldn't live through the night. I was suffering from many broken bones, severe hypothermia, and shock. Dad stayed by my side, encouraging me to hang on with all I could muster. His physical presence was an enormous buttress to death hovering over me. Dad, with a spine of iron, was bigger than life to me in those days. Somehow I gathered strength from his hard-hitting perseverance, although I know today that he was recoiling inside from the impact of my injuries. Without the relationship he once had with the Lord, he grappled over my accident with unanswered questions.

My wonderful mother passionately challenged the doctor's prognosis, and together my parents beseeched the Lord, praying that God would spare my life. Mom believed that God had a plan for me. My folks' support, gut-wrenching as it was for them, was instrumental in pulling me through my ordeal that night and the years to come.

Mom's anchor throughout her adult life was always Jesus Christ. Though it would be many years before I came to know it, the greatest legacy she left our family was her faith in Christ, refined through the furnace of a terminal illness she was diagnosed with as a young mother.

Often Mom would admonish me with a passage from God in the book of Jeremiah, *I know the plans I have for you, sayeth the Lord, plans for welfare and not for calamity to give you a future and a hope.* "God gave me this verse for you, David, when you were very young," she often reminded me. "No matter where you go or how far you run, God will always be there with you." But I simply couldn't accept that God, whoever He might be, could really care for me.

In my young adult years, she would repeat that God desires good for all of us, no matter what man may say. The fact that she was still alive at the time of my accident was a magnificent testimony of divine intervention.

As I lay in the hospital, I remembered her words, even though my thoughts were clouded by morphine and shock. *Could He really want to fulfill the desires of my heart if I would only trust in Him?* At that moment, all I desired was to walk away pain free. *What sort of a God is this?* I wondered.

I lived through a hell on Earth that night and many more nights. A break in my left humerus immediately below the shoulder left my arm paralyzed, cocked off to one side and useless. My left femur was broken in four places, one being a compound fracture. Many ribs were broken directly adjacent to my spine, as well as several vertebrae in my back. Legs that once climbed mountain slopes now lay useless in the bed. A severe concussion resulted from a fractured skull where a piece of bone was gouged from my left eyebrow. Severely swollen, my face was covered with deep lacerations, and the whites in my eyes turned blood red. The doctors put fifty-six stitches in my face to stop the bleeding.

Hours passed into days, and I began to escape the yawning mouth of hell that was demanding its toll for the injuries I'd sustained. It was a *miracle* that I lived.

Recovery was extremely slow. Multiple surgeries left my broken arm and leg in traction for weeks. The vertebrae and ribs in my back were mangled together. Distorted out of alignment and crushed, they pressed up under my skin, causing great discomfort. After close examination, the doctors considered it best to allow the bones to heal as they were.

For two months, I was forced to lie absolutely flat in the hospital bed. I was over six feet tall and barely weighed one hundred fifty pounds before this accident. As the weeks rolled by, weight that I couldn't afford to lose melted from my body, causing me to look like a bag of bones.

Lying flat brought the challenge of preventing decubiti ulcers from my heels to my head. These ulcers, or bedsores as they are often called, develop when a bony surface of the skin continually rests against a firm surface long enough to begin to cut off the blood supply. It begins with a reddening of the skin and, if left unchecked, will result in an open sore. They develop from lying or sitting in one position for any length of time. Because I was forced to lie flat on my back, decubiti ulcers first began appearing on the back of one heel and then the other, working into open sores.

It took two more months to learn to sit up and move around in a wheelchair. I fought an ongoing battle with urinary tract infections (UTIs) and bladder stones, which required more surgeries. The intense physical pain I suffered during those months in the hospital was an indescribably grim and constant jagging force that worked on my mind and soul.

Nerves had been damaged at the break in my arm near the shoulder. The doctors could not tell if I would ever regain its use. With just a hint of movement in my fingers, I tried desperately to press them into use.

Someone gave me some large marbles and challenged me to try to turn them in my hand. Gradually I improved enough that I was able to rotate two marbles in my upright palm with my thumb and little finger as my hand rested on the bed sheets. (Throughout the ensuing months, my arm and hand atrophied significantly. I lacked enough strength in my arm to even flex it at the elbow without assisting it with my right hand.) Paralysis in my left hand and arm lingered into the third month.

All through the months of recovery, I had a great deal of time to muse over my life. My dad had been a sailor during the Korean conflict. He had spent time stationed in Savanna, Cuba, and then in Philadelphia, Pennsylvania, where he came to know the Lord and participated in a Navy-Marine Gospel Mission team of enlisted men. The team traveled to various churches and presented their testimonies across Maryland, Pennsylvania, West Virginia, and Washington, DC. During this time, he met and married my mom in 1951.

She grew up in Philadelphia, one of five children. Thoughtful and full of zest, she determined to provide her children with a good life. Her heart for adventure caused her to be a bit of a romantic. For that reason, she would look forward with eager anticipation for the good in all that life threw her way. In that sense, she was a visionary.

Mom and Dad began traveling together with the Navy-Marine Gospel Mission team. With the wives of other enlisted guys, who were also newly wed, the team soon added a few young ladies singing as part of the ministry routine. Mom had a beautiful, angelic voice. Singing was her passion, and she inspired those who heard her with lasting memories.

Because of the Korean conflict, my dad was conscripted for an extra year, 1952. I was born in the naval hospital in Philadelphia on May 19 that year. When Dad's service was up, he and Mom packed everything and immediately left for the West Coast where Dad had grown up and joined the Navy. All of their worldly possessions were packed into a two-ton, twenty-three-foot travel trailer, pulled by a 1940 Chevy two-door club coupe with a 218 six-cylinder engine. Dad had purchased it from a sailor for $300. Afterward, he put $160 into it to rebuild the engine. Installing a trailer hitch that extended under the car as far as the front seat, he still found that it was not enough to bear the weight of that two-ton trailer. After calling his home in Oregon, he learned from his father, whom I always called Pop, that he might be able to find a dolly. After a few inquiries, Pop located a two-hundred-pound Nelson dolly that my Uncle Lloyd owned, and shipped it to Philadelphia. Although it distributed the weight evenly, that little Chevy was still not powerful enough to adequately pull the heavy load. Nevertheless, Dad and Mom left for the West Coast.

They had very little money, and as Dad would later say, "Every dime went toward fuel." Dad once jokingly told me, "If it took a nickel to travel around the world, we didn't have enough money to get out of sight of Philadelphia." For Mom, it was a bittersweet adventure. She was leaving her home and cultural way of life forever. On the other hand, in 1952, some folks in the urban East still believed there were wild Indians on the plains and pioneers out West. East and West cultures were still distinctly different in the fifties. Her adventuresome attitude overcame her despondency, and she set her face west like so many courageous pioneer women of the past.

In the West, her accent was as foreign as the way she perceived things. Despite her indomitable spirit, I remember for many years after we arrived in Portland, I would find her quietly sobbing with loneliness for her family. I was young and didn't understand why Mom was crying and would try to cheer her up.

During the post-WWII years, people didn't just jump in a car and drive across the continent. In places, old U.S. 30 was a one-and-a-half-lane highway in 1952. This meant that when oncoming vehicles pulling trailers approached each other, both drivers needed to hang their outside wheels off the edge of the pavement in order to safely pass.

Dad was seldom able to get the car out of second gear, so the best they could travel was 30 to 40 mph. For days on end, the car would overheat and vapor lock, requiring them to stop and let the engine cool. At that speed, it took thirty days to cross the continent. The average person didn't have a lot of money, and there weren't the facilities we have today. Mom and Dad were no different, so they camped out at night in secluded places, and ate whatever they could forage from farms along the way. Since it was August, they occasionally stopped and gleaned ears of field corn growing alongside the highway. This corn then became supper when they stopped for the night.

Throughout the trip, I was swaddled in a wicker basket lodged between the front and back seats. Children's car seats and seat belts were yet to be invented. I lay in the basket on one side of the back seat and Cindy occupied the other. Cindy would grow into a mid-size dog. At the time, we were both pups about the same age. Dad told me that Cindy, occasionally tired of looking out her side of the car, would climb into my basket to look out the other side. This, of course, caused a great commotion from deep within the basket.

Before leaving, my folks had arranged to meet Dad's folks somewhere on the plains of Nebraska. With the crude communications system in place in the early fifties, it amazed me that they actually made the rendezvous. Pop and Nana were waiting when we arrived. They were to become a solid anchor in my life, especially Pop. He had had a tough time during his childhood years, learning early the value of a man's word and of hard work. During the early forties, he and Nana, with my dad in tow, moved to Portland, Oregon, to help in the war effort. Eventually he became a truck driver. As a youngster, I always was excited to see him come home with his big truck. My boyhood imagination was full of dreams of joining him in the cab of that truck on a long trip.

Over the years, his sense of honor and integrity brought him prosperity and a lot of wisdom. He saw life as black or white. I can remember him pulling me aside many times, squaring off with me and saying, "Now, Davy, right's right and wrong's wrong, and don't you ever forget it."

Even though I was to go astray in my wilder years, those words were never far from my mind. Perhaps it was because I didn't ever want to disappoint him that I never wandered on the wrong side of the law.

Shortly after their rendezvous, while still in Nebraska, Dad's clutch went out. Dad and Pop hired a mechanic to replace the clutch, which took a few days and added more delay to the trip to Portland. Pop was driving a 1950 Hudson and traveling light. By the time they arrived in Pendleton, Oregon, he was becoming irritable from driving so slowly.

In an effort to speed the voyage along, Dad and Pop hooked the Hudson to the Chevy coupe with a tow chain. This went along well until Dad said he heard something like a gunshot. With Pop pulling our car and trailer, Dad couldn't just stop, so he asked Mom to take the wheel, and he leaned way out the door to catch sight of the wheel on the dolly. The tire had blown, causing another unwanted delay and expense.

They arrived in Portland on a Wednesday, and Dad landed job on Thursday working for $0.75 an hour. Broke, he needed work and asked if he could start on Friday, but his new boss said Monday would do. When he was in the Navy, he was earning $0.35 an hour, so this new wage seemed real good to him. After a few weeks, his boss gave him a raise to $0.85 an hour. Although that added income was high clover for him in 1952, my parents still had to watch their budget carefully. We had only one car. When Mom needed to go to town, she bundled me up and took the bus.

We lived in the trailer parked on Pop and Nana's vacant lot. My earliest memory is standing in the door of the trailer with my mom and looking out across Pop's corn patch. The memory brings up feelings of being unsettled. Looking back, I suspect that I was sensing Mom's unfulfilled longing for her family and home in a far distant place.

She bought groceries at Gilliam's Grocery Store in the Portsmouth district of Portland. She would put everything on an account there and pay it off once a week. Times were hard then, but for the most part I remember being content. Recently, Dad was talking about those times, and he ended with, "A year's a long time when you're standing on your head."

During the first few weeks, I faded between memories and reality, while lying in the hospital bed staring out the windows. Summer was in full swing when I was permitted to raise the head slightly to eat.

Finally, I was released from the Intensive Care Unit in Gresham to Emanuel Hospital in Portland. It was my only chance to be outside in a month, yet my strength had been siphoned off from the trauma I suffered. My body was so beat down, I couldn't enjoy being outside. However, this hospital was closer to my home.

In Emanuel, I worked hard to move my useless left arm and hand, beginning to have some success. Even so, it was a long and tedious process.

A doctor came into my room sometime in the late summer and told me they were going to sit me up in a wheelchair and see how I'd handle it. I was thrilled with the prospect of being out of bed. When they put me in the chair after being prone for months, however, I felt like a tube of axle grease in January being bent in the middle. I was beginning to think I had experienced every kind of pain there was to suffer, but the pain of sitting upright almost caused me to pass out.

The nurses asked me how I felt, commenting that many people lose consciousness on their first time up after having been bedridden for months. Not wanting to make a hasty retreat to the bed, I took a deep breath to clear the fog out of my head and the ringing in my ears. Turning to her, I said, "I think I can manage it okay." With that, they left me there and walked away. I was horribly uncomfortable, feeling as though I would topple forward on my face. Again I shook the cobwebs from my head, forcing myself to stay conscious.

Beyond the cobwebs stretched a foggy tunnel reaching back through time. I recalled the comforting voice of Dad reading from a large black book. After supper in the evening, a single light cast a warm hue throughout the small kitchen. Mixed aromas of fried chicken and fresh bread still hung in the air. The black book was a Bible. I couldn't understand what he was reading, but I remember it gave me a strong sense of security. Not the security from physical strength, but from strength that commanded ideas. I could sense something greater than my family and me.

Dad later told me he paid $50 for that Bible. It was a Dickson, King James Bible. He told me he couldn't buy it in any store, so he bought it from an old gentleman who had peddled door-to-door. By this time, my folks had moved into a house and were following a strict budget. That Bible was a major investment for my folks in those days. It demonstrated the importance they held in God's Word.

As I continued sitting upright, pain throbbed throughout my body. Up and down my spine, joints and muscles pulled at the mending bones and soft tissue as if to rip me apart. I battled the desire to call for help and retreat to my bed. Focusing on my past, again Mom's singing wafted through my mind.

As a young girl, she immersed herself in music. She had wanted to learn to play the piano, but her family couldn't afford such luxuries as piano lessons. Not to be stalled by finances, she taught herself to play the piano by ear. As I grew up, she would repeat, "You can always do the best you can with what you've got."

She once told us kids that she had performed in Carnegie Hall. By the time I was young enough to recognize value in music, she had become quite an accomplished pianist. Most people never knew that she couldn't read a note of music. Folks would approach her with sheet music and ask her to play it. She would say, "Oh, just hum it to me." Immediately she would pick up on the tune and begin adding chords. In minutes, she was playing the song like she had practiced it for weeks.

During my childhood, our small home was always filled with her singing. In her darkest moments, her songs rang loud and clear, driving away her despair or raising her to new heights of joy. Music inculcated my mind with a profound and mystic strength. I came to associate home, Mom, and everything warm and true with the songs I listened to during those years our home. I can still hear her singing out the words, *"Blessed assurance Jesus is mine, oh what a foretaste of glory Divine..."*

Then one day, someone gave us a piano, including a small stool with a round wobbly top, which wound up or down for height. Momentarily swaying on the stool, her misty eyes fell on the treasure before her. Clutching the keys, she began to play "The Old Rugged Cross." As she played, tears ran down her face. The feeling she played into that old hymn resonated throughout our little home. Overflowing my soul with peace, I was aware that I stood in the presence of something greater than all of life's woes.

Dad and Mom were of one mind when it came to things of God's Word. When I was young, however, Dad drifted away from the Lord. There was a conflict between him and someone in the church, causing him to stop attending services. He had his own reasons. He maintained religious convictions, but as he drifted from fellowshipping with other believers, he also drifted from the strength found in associating with true Christian men. Years would pass before the tragedy of my accident revealed to him the true source of courage and strength.

Mom took us kids to church, but I found myself losing interest in spiritual matters also. I was confused, because Dad had quit responding to God's calling. Sometimes I would sit in church and feel a desire to fill a void in me with God's mysterious power. It was that same power I once witnessed when Dad read from that big black Bible in the evenings, or when Mom filled the house with songs of praise. Confusion began to reign in my mind.

Other times I began to think that God was for women and children: just another option in life. My ideas about the world around me began to fill that void within me. Trying to marginalize any thoughts of God, I was sure He would only bring me trouble. The world offered so many intrigues, promising a glowing future of success. To accept its options, I had to free myself from religious bonds and the notion of God.

During my adolescent years I worked hard to codify this attitude. While in the process of purging religion from my thoughts, one of Mom's friends approached me after a church service and said she had had a vision of my future. She saw me on a stage in front of a church congregation. As I began to open my mouth, she could hear me preaching the gospel of Jesus Christ. I resented her words. To me she was a crazy old crone. Her revelation drove me to become even more determined to plot a life's course on the power of my strength of character, ensuring that I would have nothing to do with Christianity. Even so, I was enough of a mystic to tuck this old woman's words away in a dark corner of my mind.

The memories vanished with the nurse's arrival into my room a half hour later. I couldn't believe how washed out I felt. I had accomplished nothing more than sitting there reflecting back over the years, yet my vitality was depleted.

Sitting up in a wheelchair soon became my daily routine, bringing new pain and frustrations. As time in the chair increased, I began to move it awkwardly about the floor, visiting people I had only previously heard from my bed.

One day I bravely took the elevator down to the main floor. This was the most freedom I had experienced in months, keeping me acutely aware of how trapped I had really become.

On one rather gloomy day, I sat alone in front of the glass double doors leading out of the hospital. People were walking about, adding to my discomfort. It was a drizzly day, and rain was slowly causing little rivulets of water to run down the glass. Staring out the window, I pondered over the greater values in life. Interminable hours seemed to pass. In the glass, a strange reflection sat in a wheelchair. My deep blue eyes looked gray and hollow staring back at me. I could see right through myself as if I were empty inside. It was easy to ignore a figure without substance. As the stranger in the glass stared at me, I gazed on through the glass to the outdoors I loved, where something as simple as rain could run off freely to its destination.

My thoughts drifted off to my girlfriend Sue. She was a kindhearted girl and seemed to have a real attraction for me before this injury. Her wide blue eyes portrayed a virtue of innocence. Could she handle being with a cripple?

At five feet two inches, she was extremely attractive and very popular in her school across the river in Orchards, Washington. She had a beautiful face framed in golden hair that cascaded over her shoulders. But the sparkling joy in her eyes attracted me the most. We had been close friends for a couple of years. She made me proud when she consented to be my steady girlfriend. I longed for the closeness we had and that inner strength she carried. She was a Christian with an understanding of absolute values that puzzled me. She encouraged me to turn to Christ, but I would put her off.

Whenever she came to visit me in the hospital, it was awkward, but I was always happy she came because she transmitted her inner joy and lifted my spirit. What would she do when I was no longer hospitalized? I guessed that she would probably quietly excuse herself from my life and take up with any one of the numerous hopefuls at her school. Who could blame her? I didn't even know how to speak to her about my being confined to a wheelchair. What did I have to offer her?

Helplessly I sat and gazed through the glass at my empty reflection. Time seemed to muddle answers to my questions that mounted an unbearable pressure on me. Months can seem like years for a sixteen-year-old who feels like his hide has been turned raw side out for the world to gawk at. What had become of me, I wondered.

Although bound to a wheelchair and the hospital, I began moving in greater loops within its corridors, as I gained more physical strength. On the first floor, I discovered a small waiting room just inside a north exit to the outside world. Few people came or went through this doorway, so there was seldom anybody in this small room. I would sequester space for myself in this hideout for hours and watch out the door as the seasons advanced a day at a time without me. Summer turned to autumn, and then winter brought short, cold, gray days with clouds lingering just above the tops of the buildings.

Sometimes I would push through the doors and sit for a short time in the rain just to escape the controlled environment of the hospital. But my weakened body would pay for it the next day by being bedridden. Yet I found that the pounding of rain on my face momentarily returned me to the natural rhythmic pulse deeply rooted within me. My soul ached to recover the vanishing joy of running through the rain, heart pounding, face upward, with water dripping off my chin. I gladly traded two minutes in the rain for weeks of staring through the glass.

The constant pain I suffered in the hospital continued to intensify, as I became more active. Unless I was given some hefty pain medications, it never abated. I took several oral medications for pain, but they only masked it. So additionally, I was given four shots a day to manage pain. I no longer recall what these medications were, but they were enough to knock a grown man into a deep sleep all day. At first, they made me groggy. Within a short time, though, I felt like I was able to function without any noticeable side effects, other than relief from intense pain. In reality, I was simply learning to deal with the intoxicating grogginess.

My room in the hospital was in a ward on the fourth floor. Many people rotated through those other three beds during the months I was hospitalized. Some lived, others didn't. For weeks, a young man with severe brain trauma from a car-train collision yelled incessantly night and day whenever his medication wore down. It was disquieting. He couldn't talk, feed himself or meet any of his personal needs, yet he lived on in that helpless state, while an older gentleman in the bed next to mine slipped away during the night without a word. I was the first to discover in the morning that he'd died, and I rang for the nurse.

Life is so fragile and yet resilient at the same time. This immersed me in reoccurring questions: Why do some live through such trauma when they have so little to lose, and others die with so little effort when they have so much to gain in life? Why was I even alive?

After hearing all I'd been through, some would say, "You're lucky to be alive." My vehement thought projected itself through my reply, "If I was lucky, I'd be dead," I'd retort harshly. Yet somehow, the thought always came back like a stinging lash, and try as I could to deny it, I knew it was only by some *miracle* that I could still draw a breath.

At times, I would attempt to draw landscape pictures in an effort to unfetter my soul from the crippled body that imprisoned me. Art had always assisted me in times when I felt confined indoors before the accident. When I was younger, the pictures I drew would often attract the attention of my teachers. They would frame my work and display it in the halls. However, the severe damage to my left arm and hand was quite maddening. Combined with the paralysis of my writing hand, the imprisonment I felt seemed to smother my creative spirit. I could barely hold a pencil and wasn't able to put any pressure on the paper to vary the lead tones for contrast. Pining away, I tried to satisfy myself by concealment in the meager solitude afforded by the small waiting room downstairs.

Soon my hideout was discovered. When anyone began looking for me, that waiting room was the first place they'd look. At first, I resented being discovered because I'd usually be hauled back to the ward for some hospital routine. Yet there were times that the company was welcomed. Once my dad came down and just sat with me. He didn't say much in deference to the rare solitude that I could find. I think he understood the agony of my soul even more than I did. He used to say, "Son, I'd give anything in the world if I could trade places with you."

I knew he really meant it, which strengthened my resolve, yet I wouldn't have traded such an affliction with anyone I knew and loved. Even my worst enemy didn't warrant such a cursed exchange.

Nearly every day, my mom came to the hospital, sometimes bringing my brothers Jerry and Keith and my sister Lois. She and Lois would sit for an hour or more visiting and encouraging me, as Jerry and Keith would scurry around the room. Mom would say, "David, just because your bed has been made for you, doesn't mean you have to sleep in it." Her visits brought me hope to find a new horizon.

Others also came by in a constant flow. I had been such a recluse; I didn't even realize how many people knew I existed. Some would come and complain about their problems. Others would joke around, making me start laughing, which sent spasms of pain through my half-healed broken ribs.

Linda, a girl that I highly admired in my early years of grade school, came by to say hi to me. I hadn't seen her in years. Her sudden presence completely tongue-tied me. By the time I got over being awed by her visit and collected my words, she was gone.

Sue continued to visit me also. Whenever she came, my heart would swell with the desire to be normal. She would brighten my day. But after she left, thoughts lingered of what kind of life we could really have. I just wanted to jump up out of the sheets and run until I fell into her arms in a weary heap far, far away. I imagined us together in the deep serenity of a dark forest, sheltered from my horrific ordeal.

Many elements of hospital life bore heavily on me. Eventually I became so hungry for non-institutional food that I began groveling for people to bring me something homemade. Once Marty brought me some venison liver cooked with bacon and onions. I savored the taste, but couldn't eat it all because it was so rich. Others would smuggle in candy bars or cookies. Once, I even received the rare treat of a hot hamburger from a local restaurant known as the Oak Pit.

The flow of people with their small gifts caused me to ponder what my world was going to be like, as well as how I would get along when finally released from the hospital. Could I live by the maxim, 'When you get knocked down you get up'? These words had been ingrained in my mind from as far back as I could remember. When I was perhaps four years old, I took a tumble and came up crying. Dad said, "You're okay. Let's get you brushed off."

This maxim in my life led me to deal with affliction. Could I find the strength and courage to bear up under this tumble I'd taken and brush myself off? Like a four-year-old, I didn't even know if it was possible for *anyone* to endure such a fall.

After he put in a long day at work, Dad visited me almost every evening the entire time I was in the hospital. He would be dog-weary at times and didn't always stay long, but he made the effort to stop and visit. His perseverance and dedication to me conveyed courage under fire. Slowly his commitment during those terribly dark days taught me the values of true manhood. He always greeted me at the door with, "How are you doing, tiger?" If, on a rare occasion, he couldn't stop by, he would call. From those visits, I drew enormous strength and, most of all, a will to 'brush myself off,' so to speak, and get on with life. Wanting to be just like my dad, I didn't want to do anything to disappoint him.

When one looks back across the span of a lifetime, it sometimes feels so much richer because of the people who helped mold that life. I think my will to survive and press on was largely because I knew Dad was sacrificing the time to come when he was exhausted after a long day at work. His visits were extremely meaningful to me. The strain he and my mother must have experienced, helping me through that period of recovery and on into the ensuing years, is unimaginable to me today, and yet they persevered.

During those long months of hospitalization, I was given heart-wrenching news: I would never walk again. I felt like my guts had been ripped out of me. I was not meant for a life saddled in a wheelchair! The diagnosis paralyzed my mind, shaking the foundation of my soul. It didn't seem to be true. Initially, I knew I had a serious problem and faced months of recuperation. But this was for my entire life! My legs were part of who I was. There was no other me apart from a good healthy body. Questions swirled in my mind like a dust devil that whirled on an open plain, then ceased in a turbulent aftermath of empty silence and chaotic debris. How would I live bereft of the use of my legs? What would people think when they saw me in a wheelchair? Where would my life lead? For the time being, I decided to refuse to believe it. There was nothing I couldn't overcome if I had the determination to triumph over my problems. I was caught in a maelstrom of unrelenting concerns, demanding answers that would chart my future.

In the meantime, I started a homeschool study program in the hospital. The routine activity of school added a new dimension to the storm of life I wasn't prepared to face. As a loner, I wasn't ready to face going back to school. The harsh reality brought too many unanswered questions that swept through my mind like endless echoes trapped in a box canyon. I needed time to think through my circumstances. Pondering my future was difficult. How could I respond to questions from a curious crowd when I possessed no answers? Needless to say, I was very confused. In any case, my injury caused me to grow up and think about life as a man much faster than I expected as a teenager.

My biggest blessing at that time was that my paralyzed left arm gradually regained strength. Finally, I was able to thrust myself out of my chair on the parallel bars in the physical therapy department. I exercised on those bars daily, bringing strength to my arms and shoulders. I also continued rotating the marbles in my hand to exercise my fingers. As my body healed, I became restless. The restlessness provoked an intense desire to go home.

So, in October, the doctor began authorizing weekend passes for me to spend at home. They allowed me to leave on a Friday evening and return Sunday or Monday morning. These passes gave me the opportunity to slowly break into a normal life pattern. It also gave those around me an understanding of what I would need when I was released from the hospital.

Although I received physical therapy, this treatment didn't help me understand how my new life in a wheelchair would fit into the world I knew. Learning to open and close doors, move around furniture, cook food, wash dishes, or even take a drinking glass from an upper cupboard were all new challenges. Everything needed rethinking. Furthermore, those around me needed to adjust to having a wheelchair invade their living space.

I was so grateful to be home, even if it was for a few days. But weekends at home really wore me out. The pain I suffered didn't seem to be diminishing with my increased activities, so my use of narcotics continued. Additionally, I continued to suffer from UTIs (urinary tract infections), and there were more surgeries to abate those problems. In spite of all these challenges, I was really ready to be away from the hospital altogether.

Once I tasted home-cooked meals, I kept pressing the issue of staying at home. Finally, one of the doctors told me I could leave the hospital when I was not so dependent on pain medication. For the most part, I'd weaned myself from powerful shots, but was very dependent on narcotic pills. I wanted to go home so badly that the next day I refused any pain medication. The nurses asked me if I was in any kind of pain. Equivocating, I told them I'd be okay. Living without the pain medication was horrific at first. Every time I moved, waves of pain traveled down my spine into my feet. I was determined to go home, though. If that's what it took, I was also determined to live with the pain.

After five months in the hospital and several weeks of monitoring me off the pain medication, I finally received a doctor's release from the hospital altogether. Five months can also be a long time for a sixteen-year-old standing on his head. Thanksgiving of 1968 would be in a few days.

For years afterward, I carried a foam pad wherever I went. I placed it in the middle of my back at the site of the break. There were so many bones that were broken without being reset that after the swelling abated, they thrust up under my skin like a bag of golf balls along my spine. Whenever I reclined in my chair or lay flat in bed, the pad reduced the pain to a tolerable level of discomfort. It also helped prevent my skin from becoming sore at that spot.

Pain remained a constant companion that often set my teeth on edge, but I forced myself to live with it. After quitting the powerful pain-killing drugs, I lost all desire to use them again. Over time, I simply built up a tolerance to the pain and finally reached a point where I even discontinued the use of the foam pad. Often when the pain became overbearing, I'd swing my useless legs over the edge of the bed and then using my arms, swing into my chair to stretch.

Decubiti ulcers over my ischial spine where I sat threatened me daily. To reduce the potential of forming these ulcers, I learned to awaken myself frequently at night to shift position. Furthermore, I continued to suffer from UTIs regularly.

Although I know today that God's watchful eyes were on me, guiding me every step of the way during my hospitalization and the months that followed, I couldn't see it back then. There were so many challenges to face and obstacles to overcome. Often I felt life was not worth living. Initially, I thought God, whoever He was, had cursed me for denying Him. I was sure He was fed up with me, feeling no desire to help me. With flawed reasoning, I felt my reckless life had finally brought me what I deserved. But this was the furthest thing from the truth. I know now that even during those times, God heard my humble prayers questioning who He was. I'll elaborate more on this in my next book.

Like many defining moments in life, this event sent me careening unprepared for the life that lay ahead. I was sure it no longer had any value. No longer did I possess the strength of my youth, or the ability to be independent. I would never again stand straight as a man should stand. I viewed myself as a half-man, and a half-man is no man. These thoughts played havoc in my mind. To top all this off, I found myself barred from the mountains where I could be alone. My life had come to a dead-end road of misery and constant agony.

I have lived long enough to recognize that everybody has had some degree of unexpected troubles, often deep, abiding troubles that go unseen by those around us, such as a heart condition or even an abusive relationship. There can be dark, abiding mental disorders that cripple the mind, sending a person into the abyss of despair, or emotional struggles leaving a person's soul paralyzed with a sense that they are worthless.

Still others may believe that their whole life has been slammed into a brick wall, and all their plans lie in a heap of rubble.

Although these things can mold habits, they do not have to define character. Rather, it's how we live with our troubles that makes the difference and defines our character. A person must seize what's at hand in any given circumstance. To live to our potential, we must realize that circumstances will often create a new normal in our lives. No one will deny that accepting this is difficult, but adversity can be overcome. Unexpected suffering and misfortune usually occur at the most inconvenient time; a time that no one would choose as appropriate. These spontaneous eruptions trouble and torment our lives as well as those around us. What makes the difference is what we do when those difficulties or troubles come our way.

Jim Caviezel put it this way in the 2002 movie, *The Count of Monte Cristo*. Caviezel, playing the part of Edmond Dantes, makes a toast to the younger Mondego:

> *"Life is a storm, my young friend. You will bask in the sunlight one moment, be shattered on the rocks the next. What makes you a man is what you do when that storm comes. You must look in that storm and shout as you did in Rome, 'Do your worst! For I will do mine!' Then the fates will know you as we know you...Albert Mondego, the man."*

CHAPTER THREE

Brushing the Dust Off While Gripping the Hurricane Deck

A guy once asked me, "What was the worst thing you remember about the accident that put you in a wheelchair?"

An undercurrent of memories ripped through my mind, stinging me like a hot lash. I stared at the ground, contemplating an answer. Actually, the worst things never passed. Problems with bed sores and ulcers were an ongoing battle. My arm continued to suffer from the lingering effect of paralysis, although it was gradually recovering. I regarded constant pain a familiar companion. Then, there was that deep agonizing emptiness tearing at my soul saying, "You are not supposed to be in a wheelchair!" Day after day, I groaned inwardly, living hopelessly chained in bondage by the words, "You will never walk again."

For a long moment, I stared at my useless legs. I couldn't share all that in a moment's reply. Gazing up at the guy, I quipped with a gleam in my eye that belied my hidden agony, "When I hit the bottom." Despite the jest, this was literally, as well as figuratively, true. Hitting bottom was the worst part of the accident and of my life as well. Behind many smiles, there are tears.

Many people have lived through terrible circumstances that have resulted in crippling conditions much worse than mine. Some, like mine, are obvious at a glance. Others suffer with afflictions that are insensible to the casual onlooker. In every case, all have paid a high price in hardships. Some of those burdens are so horrific they are difficult to bear alone. Over many years, I have learned to endure mine by the grace of God. Ultimately it's been the only way I could do it over the long haul. In the end I hope to have wrested my full measure out of life despite my circumstances. After all, what is it to a man with a heart, soul, and mind if he never explores his limits?

Today, my greatest desire is that God will be glorified when others witness the spiritual strength God has given me to pursue dauntlessly His plan in my life. Admittedly, living at the edge of my limits with the strength given to me takes courage. Courage is not easy to come by, yet God offers it to those who will invite Him into their lives.

My mother exemplified this to me. She was never in the public light, yet she touched the lives of hundreds of people. From an early age, she had trouble breathing. A series of childhood pulmonary diseases left her with bronchiectasis, a chronic destruction of the lungs that is treatable with antibiotics today. In the days before antibiotics, however, it had a grim prognosis. By the time antibiotics became available to her, the damage had become an irreversible degenerative condition.

As a child, she didn't complain, drawing in each breath and savoring it. Over the years, breathing became more difficult, building in her a unique sort of character. One day, as a young woman, she discovered the One who gave her the air she breathed and the strength to draw each breath. In gratitude to her Savior, her life became His. In the faith given her by God, she discovered hope, and in hope each new breath. With each one, she saw blessings in her life that escaped the notice of others. Despite her lung condition, she developed a passion to sing. As is often the case, things that bring people the most joys are thwarted by frustrations from personal imprisonment. Despite them, she pressed toward her potential and *sang*.

She committed her life to its fullest for Jesus. By learning to control her breathing, she was able to lift her singing to heights not dreamed. Another breath brought marriage; another brought children. Breathing began to be a labor until, in her early twenties, she was told she was dying. To slow the process, the doctors undertook a dangerous surgery for those days and removed part of her lung. Despite the extra time she was given, she was told she would never see her children grow to maturity.

With one slow breath, she sought the One she had learned to depend upon even more than doctors. With another breath, faith became indomitable courage. With yet another, my youngest brother Keith was born. With his arrival, she had four children.

Other children from around the neighborhood gravitated to her doorstep. Mom loved children: to teach them a song, tell them a scary story, or spin a yarn. But whether telling spooky stories to wide-eyed children on the front porch in the hot summer evenings or masterminding neighborhood parades in Red Flyer wagons on our dead-end road, she always put her faith in action, as she labored in her breathing. The impact she had on the lives of many children certainly was not dead-ended.

Music of praise to God ascended from her damaged lungs. It was a central part of her life, and so it became part of mine. Through songs, she shared the love and joy for God she held in her heart.

Nights were often the worst for her. Coughing fits brought blood, and the lonely hours of darkness screeched, "You haven't much time left now!" Yet in the howling chasm of empty fear, a still small voice emerged stronger. *"Trust in the Lord with all your heart and lean not unto your own understanding."* When the dawn of each new morning appeared, she would utter prayers of thanksgiving for the fresh breaths she could draw.

She trusted God deeply for a blessing we all have, yet few of us ever appreciate. Upon that, she built a godly heritage for her children and grandchildren, teaching us how we could trust and have faith in Christ Jesus for ourselves. As it was, in the process, her very profound message of a deep abiding faith slowly transferred into a future that she was not expected to see.

Get her laughing, and she sounded like a chicken cackling, as she used all her strength to heave in one deep breath to release yet another series of cackles! Her laughter was infectious. We loved to share in her laughter. Although it strained her breathing, most people didn't notice. Being the oldest child, I saw that within her laughter, her heart seemed to mock something dark and sinister that threatened her. Yet she never brought it up, and we were nearly oblivious to the force that menaced her. She would gulp in one last hilarious breath to heave out a final round of laughter. With that breath, a gleam in her eyes flashed her deep dependence on God; *"In all your ways acknowledge Him and He will direct your path."*

More breaths, slower with added labor, brought grandchildren and then great grandchildren. But they didn't notice the labor. She didn't wear it on the outside. Life and the Breath of Life were a more important message to her than her impending departure from this world. She lived each day with the real knowledge that each breath was a gift on the wings of borrowed time. Eventually, she became 'Gramma Ellie' to numerous grandchildren the doctors once swore she'd never see. No one ever owned the name 'Gramma Ellie' with more pride. There was One giving her time, and she wanted her grandchildren to know Him and the joy and happiness He had for them. *"I know the plans I have for you sayeth the Lord, plans for welfare and not for calamity to give you a future and a hope."* As she claimed this Scripture for others, she learned to cherish and own it even deeper within the sanctuary of her own heart.

The doctors were amazed, as she grew older. Having outlived her life expectancy, she lived with a youthful disregard for her age. With this attitude, she enchanted and mystified young and old alike, boldly proclaiming from God's Word, *"This is the day that the Lord has made, we will be glad and rejoice in it!"* As such, she spread the joy that God gave her from the West Coast to the East, and from the Rocky Mountains to the Great Basin, and then to Alaska in hopes that everyone she knew would enjoy life eternal with her one day. With loved ones at soccer games, summer picnics, Christmases at Gramma's, long walks on the beach or through sagebrush hills, and even sledding down a mountain slope 'lickety-split,' life was a long enchanting moment of succeeding breaths never taken for granted.

I have become strong by standing on the shoulders of giants like Mom. Many people, triumphing over insurmountable odds, go before us as living examples, inspiring us as examples of how we might live our life heavily encumbered by debilitating conditions. These people have lived and survived not by the way they have wanted their life to be, but by a hidden strength to overcome insurmountable difficulties. For me, this strength was found in the simple courage of acknowledging that I was blessed by what I had.

It is hard for any of us to be thankful for what we have in the face of immense suffering and loss. However, though I'd lost the use of my legs, still I'm blessed with two strong arms. To be able to move a hand or finger, to see and hear, to be able to talk or share a smile are all in and of themselves blessings. It's only when we have the courage to accept what we have been blessed with, and to stop focusing on what we struggle against that we can reach our potential, making a difference in the lives of others. By seizing this courage, people who have determined to live up to their potential and strive toward goals, have won great victories. Furthermore, they have sacrificed their lives as beacons of hope for countless others, as I can hope to offer mine.

I don't fully understand why the human experience is riddled with troubles. There are no simple answers to why bad things happen to people, and I offer no explanation. In the economy of human understanding, life is simply not fair. My heart is so heavily burdened at times with the disabilities and struggles of others that it nearly drives me to tears. I stand in awe of their ability to cope with difficulties unimaginable to me.

Yet I know that there is One who cares about our deepest burdens. Jesus cares about the dreadful anguish that some have endured throughout their lives. To those suffering from the effects of demoralizing distress, He offers peace. He holds out nail-pierced hands for those tortured by struggle. The Man of Sorrows offers comfort to those paralyzed by agonizing grief. To those who live in pain, He offers hope from a face beaten and scarred by thorns. Strength and courage are available to those who earnestly seek it from the Source of life.

In the span of more than half a century, I've found that the power to overcome insurmountable difficulties, to deal with unwanted circumstances, and to thrive in the desolate wilderness of severe, soul-devastating disability may be found in Jesus Christ. God Himself, through Jesus Christ, joins us in our solitude and emptiness to give abundant life and courage if we will only believe.

When I first broke my back, I couldn't see all these things that I see now, so I fought against accepting Christianity. To me, God was a crutch for the weak-hearted. Believing my difficulties could be overcome on my own strength, I pressed onward alone, attempting to forge my life. I had developed a self-reliant attitude that drove me to despise any spiritual help. Even so, I secretly loathed the prospect of life confined to a wheelchair.

Well-minded people seemed only to antagonize me. They intensified hopelessness toward my future. They would say, "You can become an accountant," or "You might consider a drafting job." They might as well have told a healthy, active thirty-year-old merchant marine to join the quilting club, chatting with the ladies over a cup of tea. Those little bits of advice killed hope. Consequently, I began to develop distaste for people who saw me only as crippled man.

Additionally, I saw some unknown god as the source of my problems. The god of my imagination could have prevented the accident or healed me, and he didn't. My antipathy toward that god drove me to want nothing that might place me even remotely in his shadow. So ultimately I rejected the only true God. Frustrated, I wondered what value there could be in a crippled life oppressed by stereotypes and abandoned by God. To compound it all, sitting in a wheelchair felt alien. Operating the contraption seemed worse. Determined to escape these things, I would go so far as destroying myself, if necessary. Life at that time was a terrible conundrum.

To me, it is amazing how the true God will meet us when we loathe Him or won't even acknowledge His existence. Reflecting back to those months in the hospital, I recalled one afternoon when my wheelchair sat by the side of my bed. Cold and silent as a tombstone, its silent screams echoed an empty epitaph of my future life. It was a thing of revulsion.

About that time, I remember meeting a man perhaps in his early thirties. He seemed to stroll into my room, as though he were on a mission with a clandestine motive. I wanted to be alone, beyond the reach of those enthusiastic to help the cripple. Instantly, I saw a prosthetic on his arm and another on his leg. I was feeling glum about my circumstances, as he stopped next to my bedside, introducing himself. After some brief small talk, he pulled my empty chair toward him. "If you're going to get along in life, you'll need to learn to operate this thing." That said, he sat in my wheelchair, and then in a single stroke, thrust it back on two wheels, spun it in circles, and walked it forward and backward on two wheels.

Thunderstruck, I stared at him, doing calisthenics in my chair. Where a strong right hand had once been, he bore a hook. Fixed firmly in the spokes, he deftly used it, as the chair responded in smooth motion to his bidding. That repulsive piece of upholstery and metal suddenly became a vehicle of graceful elegance, as if hovering in the air over the floor. My mouth must have been agape, for he flashed a smile. Dropping the front wheels back gently to the ground, he spoke as if continuing his sentence, "It's the only way you'll get down and back over curbs to cross the streets."

Suitably impressed, I wondered, *how'd you do that?* I no longer remember his name; perhaps he was an angel in disguise. But I could not help but realize what a turning point he brought to me that day. He spoke a few encouraging words and disappeared from my life as mysteriously as he arrived, never to be seen again. Today, from my present stage of life, I thank God for bringing him into my room at just that perfect moment.

In the 1960s, dipped curbs to assist people in wheelchairs were rare. Armed with this new information, I focused on how I might overcome at least some minor obstacles. I felt that if I concentrated on handling small problems, perhaps the greater ones wouldn't loom so large. Because I was raised to make do with what I had, I never felt entitled to be helped by someone else. There was no reason to believe that the world should adapt to me. So, from that visit, I decided to do my best to adapt to the world around me. I began to formulate an unrelenting idea in my mind that if the wheelchair could go over curbs, it might also operate in the woods. Although nobody ever showed me how to get over a curb, this guy gave me a glimmer of hope. Until he dropped by, I didn't even know the front wheels of my chair might come off the ground without killing me. The thought of spending my life enslaved to a smooth surface had been my miserable outlook. Suddenly an entirely new world began to emerge.

There is a death worse than dying. That is the death of hope. My heart aches for those who live without hope. Hope is an asset for those who find it. Those who do will have courage to go on with life, despite life's terrible predicaments. Armed with hope, they can ride out and surmount difficulties, tenaciously hanging on to their own hurricane decks in life. Hope and courage to say, *'Do your worst! For I will do mine!'* and then look at life with eager anticipation.

This is not to say living in a wheelchair is easy. It was a horrific adjustment. There have been many difficulties, and they continue to this day. But I choose not to allow them to be the focus of my life. Indeed, hope has brought challenging adventures, as I've tested my limits.

Admittedly, the hope to overcome ridiculous odds has given me some precarious rides, for lack of a good pair of legs. But those rides have served only to quicken the pulse of my life, spurring me on with the courage to seek greater hope in tomorrow.

By choosing to focus on the adventure of living, I eventually found freedom. Pericles once said, '*The secret to happiness is freedom, the secret to freedom is a brave heart.*' Courage brings happiness. To me, the courage to press on, to struggle against confining circumstances, is the virtue of life. It's where we discover our true potential.

The Bible tells us that "*by whatever a man is overcome, by this he is enslaved.*" To the best of my ability, I have learned not to allow my chair to enslave me. Instead, I have been able to live within the full potential of my limits with all the strength that God gives me. Yes, I realize everybody's limits are different. Some people do indeed endure much greater hardships than I could ever imagine. Some burdens are much greater to bear than others. Everyone, however, can live to their full potential in the strength and grace God has to offer.

A wise old gentleman once told me, "Everyone packs a different load of moose!" *Okay,* I pondered, after seeing how a double amputee could overcome his condition, *I'll learn to pack what load of moose I can carry, a little at a time. That made sense.*

First, I needed to do what my angel fellow showed me. Get this chair up on two wheels. So, I began to practice. Immediately, during this stage of wheelchair 101, I also had to learn to get back into the 'saddle' when the wheelchair bucked me out backward. Up and down and out I went until I began to be its master.

While sitting in a mall one day, I kicked the chair back and balanced it perfectly still on two wheels to ease the pain in my back. A man passing by blurted out, "Whoa! Have you ever gone over backward doing that?"

Nonchalantly I responded, "Not lately." That comment brought a rewarding smile from him.

During the ensuing months, I received very little of the kind of sympathy that would encourage me to feel sorry for myself. Dad always said, "You play with the cards dealt to you."

Once I was mouthing off to my mom, assuming that I could get away with it because I was confined to a wheelchair. Unfortunately for me, I was practicing my balancing act at the same time. Before I knew it, she spun around, hooking her foot under the footrest of my chair and flipped it over backward with me in it!

"Hey!" I hollered. "You can't do that!"

"Yes, I can," she gently replied. "Now get yourself up and think about your mouth while you're doing it." After that, I was careful not to engage in confrontations propped up on two wheels.

Combined with practicing my balancing technique on two wheels, I learned to move forward on them across rough ground. In fact, I soon learned that if I even tried to descend a steep hill on rough ground with all four wheels on the ground, the small front wheels would hang up and the chair would buck forward. So, traveling on four wheels was not always an option. In the meantime, I was getting pretty cock sure of myself.

At one point, my brother Jerry and I were going down to a set of corrals from a mess hall at camp. A road swung around to the east on a gentle grade, while a shortcut trail was incised straight down the mountain in front of us. Jerry headed for the road, but I stopped and examined the trail.

Turning back, he retorted, "Com'on."

I hesitated, then quietly answered, "Let's go this way. It's shorter."

Jerry stood at the top of the trail. Then he looked at me like I was crazy. "Can you do that?"

"Sure," I responded confidently, although I had never done anything that irrational before. Then kicking the chair up on two wheels, I cautiously spilled over the edge. My wheels straddled either side of the incised trail and Jerry filed in behind me. It was late in the summer and hadn't rained for awhile. The trail was about fifty yards long and dusty. Each time Jerry put his foot down, dust puffed up around his boot. The farther I went, the more confident I became, so I began to gain speed.

About three quarters of the way to the bottom, the trail widened to where my wheels were in the dust. I could hear my brother trotting along behind me. Although I was wearing gloves, the heat built up from the friction of the rubber on my gloved hands. If I loosened my grip to relieve the heat, the chair went faster. Dust began to shoot off the back of my tires like a rooster tail, while Jerry continued pounding the ground behind me. It must have been quite a sight.

Suddenly my left wheel dropped into a hole covered over with fine dust. I quickly learned the chair could buck sideways and forward at the same time. I tried to catch my balance by dropping the front wheels to the ground, but doing that carried its own set of problems. The chair and I took a few tumbles before I separated from it. Coming to a stop at the bottom of the hill, the chair rested on my crumpled frame.

When Jerry arrived, he pulled the chair off me, as I brushed the dust from my hair and spit it out of my mouth. My clothing was now a dusty tan, but all my parts were still connected in the right places. "Are you alright?"

"Yes," I answered a bit uncertain. "I think so."

Thinking he would say something like, 'wow, that was quite a ride,' he instead replied "Alright." Then he turned and continued toward the corral, as though I was any other guy that had just taken a spill out of recklessness, leaving me to collect my own load. Once again I discovered stupid hurts!

You've heard that life takes place where the rubber meets the road. Well, for me, life takes place where the rubber meets the ball of my hand, and I have the calluses to prove it! Every one of them is well earned.

The backcountry in which I have lived since my accident is still wild and rough and has not yet been introduced to handicapped awareness programs. So, crossing it in a wheelchair has, at times, been like riding the hurricane deck over a savage land. During some of those occasions, I have entertained myself quite unexpectedly with my own personal rodeo. When spontaneous eruptions occur beneath me, it's usually debatable which of us will come out on top, the wheelchair or me.

On one such occasion, I was crossing through a muddy corral headed for the gate after a bunch of us had been riding horses. The guys I was with had headed for the house. I was alone. Our horses were tied to a hitching rail adjacent to the shed wall. The driest place to walk was between the hitching rail and the shed. As I have often discovered, though, the best route to travel is also the narrowest, prohibiting travel by wheelchair. Finding the mud deeper toward the center of the corral, I tried to hug close to the back of the horses and mule. I knew better, but as it has been said before, good judgment comes from bad experiences and, well, experience brings about wisdom. In any case, I would soon be weighed in the balance against the better part of wisdom, and found lacking.

I passed by the first gentle horse without the reward of feeling its hind feet. Thus, I threw discretion to the wind. After all, I was in a wheelchair. Surely the mule would have compassionate understanding. The mule was not going to have any part of my indiscretion, however. He wasn't disciplined by popular 'sensitivity' training. A normal mule has the tendency to think with its feet when it objects to people being indiscreet around it. This one happened to be normal. Catching me broadside with both feet, it sent me and my hurricane deck into the center of the corral where good judgment would have directed me in the first place. The worst of the situation was not that I was kicked. I deserved that. But it was that the wheelchair arrived there first, imperiling my safe landing.

When my hurricane deck begins to 'catch air,' I'm just as equally liable to get hurt real bad as the next guy. Therefore I've always felt I was equal to any man. Being handicapped means there's something a person might not be able to experience as well as someone else and may need some help. However, I have found that my body has experienced an equal share of bruises, cuts, scratches, and broken bones as the next guy. Looking back, I've discovered that I've needed no help obtaining these inflictions. Hence I have often told people that I'm not handicapped; I'm crippled. Please overlook the fact that I'm not politically correct. In saying this, I'm simply acknowledging the fact that there are people who are far worse off than I am.

As I recovered from my injuries in 1968, I began to seriously apply myself to my studies. Returning to school my senior year was another difficult adjustment. I obviously wasn't normal in the sense that the average run-of-the-mill student would consider normal. Many of the students either ignored me or fell all over me, trying to help me accomplish things I could do for myself. There didn't seem to be any middle ground. I was okay with being ignored, for then people left me alone. But having students and faculty fall all over me conspicuously placed me in a very uncomfortable light. It was as if they felt that somehow or other the paralysis of my lower extremities also damaged the area above my shoulders.

Granted, I didn't get the best grades in school before my accident because I was absent from school so much of the time. Maintaining a steady effort toward my academic future, I began to receive A's and B's in my studies. With better grades, I started feeling good about where I was going academically. I resented being made to feel stupid by well-meaning people who naively assumed my paraplegia affected my mind.

Looking toward college, I found my high school counselor viewed me through the same stereotype as many others. He assumed I couldn't work toward a degree in one of the earth sciences because I was bound to a wheelchair. Later, in college I encountered the same attitude barriers. All I could do in defense was to concentrate on getting high grades in what education I needed, then pursue private extra-curricular studies. This response, however, spawned an even greater tendency in my mind to marginalize people.

While working against the attitudes of those who viewed my condition according to the conventional wisdom of the times, I continued adjusting to the paralysis in my legs and the ever-present pain. With my left arm gaining new strength each day, my desire to drive increased. I purchased a 1963 Oldsmobile Cutlass in the spring of 1969. It was a two-door sedan with an automatic transmission. Receiving a set of hand controls, I reasoned how they worked and installed them in the car. Ironically, when I went to drive the car the first time, my instinctive impulse was to use my foot to stop the car. After nearly running into a wall, I realized that I needed to rewire my brain.

Next I locked the wheelchair brakes, placing one hand on the chair and one on the car seat and made an educated guess how to swing into the car. I have long since derived some benefit from the knowledge that brakes on a wheelchair are completely relative to the position of the chair. For example, when the chair is upside down, the brakes keep the wind only from making the wheels spin like a whirlybird. When that happens, the brakes are completely ineffective toward fixing its location to the surface of the earth.

My strategy to swing into the car sounded pretty simple, rehearsed in my mind, but when it came to carrying out the plan, I learned a new lesson. In the void between the chair and car, the wheelchair took on a new center of gravity. I soon discovered being suspended in that void was a poor place to learn the practical application of Newton's third law of motion. While swinging over to the car, the center of the chair's gravity shifted to the front wheels, which *didn't* have brakes. With the chair moving away from the car, my arms stretched out as if preparing to fly. Somehow I knew this wasn't going to be a soft landing. Needless to say, I was glad for all the practice I had learning to get from the ground back into the chair.

After learning to enter and exit the car, I began working out the details of loading the baggage. Folding the wheelchair, I leaned the seat of the two-door car forward and pulled the chair into the backseat area behind me. Even after I became proficient at it, the whole process was tedious. Quite often the chair would hang up, as I pulled it in or out from behind the seat. This provided me ample opportunity to carry out some rather hostile aggression against it. Eventually this accomplishment gave me freedom to escape into the hills outside of Portland.

By this time, I longed to breathe free in the high country. Immersed in my car, I withdrew from people even more. Fortunately for me, my car insisted on pretending it was a pickup truck. I desperately needed to remove myself from the most traveled roads, and my car agreed. Consequently, in the first couple of years, I went through three gas tanks in one car. That car found it irresistible to pass a two-track road that wound away from the more traveled roads. Whenever I left town, it insisted on taking me into some rough places.

The radio reception wasn't very good outside of cities in the 1960s. During the long drives, I began to look for ways to entertain myself. My mind would wander off to tales I'd read about the wild northlands. These tales had stirred my imagination since my youth. The poet Robert Service wrote ballads of the men and women who had settled the North. While I was still quite young, I discovered I had an aptitude for memorization. As I wandered farther from home, I began to memorize many of his ballads. Although my car radio was beyond reception, the wheels hummed freedom's song. Together we sang, or I'd recite ballads aloud to her accompaniment, as we traveled the lonely backcountry. Often these ballads took on an eerie life of their own near *a lone firelight*, as the car silently listened in the flickering shadows.

While becoming accustomed to mastering a wheelchair, I took a full-time job in the spring of 1970, just past my eighteenth birthday and nearly two years after the accident. The Bureau of Land Management (BLM), Division of Engineering, hired me as a cartographic aide. The Portland Service Center, where I worked, conducted technical services for Nevada, California, Oregon, Idaho, and Washington BLM offices. My job was to help prepare planometric maps in these states. I pored over these maps, making an imprint of mountains, valleys, rivers, and roads in my mind.

Some of that wild country I found too irresistible to examine simply on paper. On weekends, I explored the country I had mapped during the week. Many of the roads I detoured onto were more suitable for a four-wheel-drive vehicle. Nevertheless, my car assured me she could travel them and navigate around the ruts and rocks.

Fleeing to the open spaces re-ignited my passion to seriously resume my skills on canvas. Exploring different art media, such as pen and ink, charcoal pencils, oil, and acrylic paints, brought much satisfaction. Sequestered away, the hours would roll past me like rivers on sunny days of long ago. As I immersed myself into my artwork, I began to feel torn between two jealous mistresses. On one hand were the wide, open spaces, and on the other, my imagination to reproduce those wild places from the hidden recesses of my mind. Lustfully, I fell into the clutches of both, allocating them much of my free time.

In town, I was learning to maneuver around in the city. Having mastered balancing on two wheels, I began tempting fate by jumping off curbs while balanced on my back wheels. I found if I could get enough forward momentum going on two wheels, I could jump curbs and get back on the sidewalks after I crossed the street. The trick was to keep the front wheels off the ground long enough that they would come down *on* the sidewalk and roll. As the back wheels were forced to follow, the forward momentum carried the whole chair over the curb and up onto the sidewalk. That's how it worked under normal circumstances.

Whenever normal circumstances failed to occur in the given order, another wheelchair rodeo usually resulted. Occasionally, I couldn't keep those front wheels up, and they would drop just before the curb, allowing only the footrest of the chair to reach the sidewalk. My high speed approach would come to an abrupt halt, causing a storm beneath me. Then I could easily find myself over the curb minus the chair. To avoid this unfavorable separation (which always causes great commotion among bystanders), I learned to quickly hook my arm around the back of my chair. This eliminated the horrified reaction of onlookers who couldn't cope with a guy in a wheelchair, plastering himself on the sidewalk.

Wheelchairs in the 1960s were clearly not designed for the vigorous use I demanded of them. My dad, a machinist in his earlier years, had taught me to use his equipment at an early age to machine parts and weld breaks as they occurred. This came in handy, as my chairs deteriorated. Keeping spokes in the wheels presented more challenges. Whenever I would acquire a new chair, I would rethread the wheels with heavy-gauge spokes. Even so, I was constantly breaking and replacing them.

Stairs always seemed to pop up in the most inconvenient places. When they did, I usually had to backtrack to find a way around them. This became rather annoying. My experience with curbs made me think stairs were only a series of curbs, so why not go up on two wheels and bounce down them like I did off a curb. This untested rationalization seemed sound, except for one unforeseen flaw. At the bottom of a curb is a broad flat surface; at the bottom of a step is something called the tread. A tread is designed for feet, not wheels. If this tread is not deep enough to rest a large wheel, it will naturally slide down on to the next step and so on until it reaches the bottom. I soon discovered that a wheelchair—unrestrained by backup assistance—would bounce like a ball down a flight of steps when the treads were too narrow. As for the occupant of the chair, this law of physics was destined to have the same effect.

I don't remember who was with me the first time I wrestled with a flight of stairs. It may have been my sister Lois. From atop that short flight of stairs, I kicked the chair back on to two wheels and let her buck! Scrambling to keep from going over forward on my face and leaving a reminder of my intrepid hide on the stairs became an immediate preoccupation. My feet left the footrest, and my legs flailed about in the air, as my hat took flight. I'm sure there was daylight showing on the seat where I normally reposed, and I was grabbing for whatever I could find to pull the hurricane deck back underneath me. By the time I hit the bottom of the stairs, I had bounced so much that I overshot some steps without even touching them, but I actually came to rest with the chair still beneath me. I have tackled many stairs since that time. Bouncing down most, I have been much more successful than that first trip.

The major drawback to stairs was a shorter life cycle for spokes. I constantly had to remove tires and rethread spokes into my wheels. Eventually I learned to be sure that the tread on the stair steps was wide enough so that I could pause between steps. This saved me a great deal of bouncing around, and a lot of spokes. If the treads were not wide enough, I learned to weigh the consequences with a little more wisdom and screw my hat down tighter.

Perhaps a year after my accident, Dad and I decided to go to the Oregon coast during an exceptionally low tide to dig for clams. We loaded our gear in the pickup, hooked up the boat trailer, and left for Tillamook Bay several hours before daylight. When we arrived, a large portion of the bay area was drained, and the tide was still going out, leaving the floor of the bay exposed. After finding a location along a northern river draining into the bay, we launched the boat and navigated through a maze of estuaries to the exposed bottom of the bay.

Daylight was breaking, and many people were out clamming. With my clamming shovel across my lap, we headed out to dig clams. We were approximately in the center of the bay on its exposed bottom on slightly higher ground. Enjoying the time together, we were having great success filling our clamming bag. Shortly after sunrise, the tide began to come in, slowly filling the bay. As the water level rose, people around us moved back to their boats to vacate the area. We kept an eye on our boat and occasionally Dad, aided by the rising tide, would move it closer to where we were digging.

On his last jaunt back to the boat, he found the incoming tide had filled a small estuary full of water, isolating me from the boat. It was narrow enough that he could jump across, but not deep enough yet to float the boat. I had no intention of wading across it in my chair. By then, most of those clamming folks had left the area.

Upon his return, Dad told me I could keep digging if I wanted to, and he'd go back and get the boat. The plan was that when the tide raised the water level, he'd float up alongside me and pick me up. So, off he went, leaving me alone. Folks meandering by warned that the tide was coming in and asked if I needed any help getting back to shore. Armed with a good plan and not alarmed by the incoming tide, I simply told them no, offering no further explanation. Soon I was isolated from everyone. Folks began hollering across estuaries of rising water with dire warnings to leave.

The tide continued creeping closer to my position, but it was still too shallow to float a boat across. In the meantime, I could see Dad keeping watch over me a short distance away. At last, I was sitting on a piece of ground too small to cuss a cat. With the water rising, a gentle breeze blew in from the Pacific. A small group of cars and people accumulated along the highway a couple miles away at the shoreline, pointing in my direction and watching through binoculars. About this time, I began to see the humor in the entire situation. Here I was, a guy in a wheelchair ostensibly alone out in the middle of the bay. All evidence to those onlookers seemed to indicate I'd been abandoned to a watery fate. Soon the little piece of ground disappeared, enveloped by the incoming tide. To keep my feet dry, I picked them up and rested them on the leg pads of my chair. There I sat in lonely glory, shovel and clam bag across my lap, with not a sight of land between the edge of the bay and me.

Thankfully, cell phones weren't invented yet. Surely one of those folks in the growing crowd worrying along the shore would have had the United States Coast Guard on its way to rescue me. There certainly was an escalation of frenzied commotion along the north side of the bay. By the time I began to feel the tidal current flowing through the spokes of my wheels, Dad had pulled up alongside me with the boat. Smiling down at me, he asked if I might be interested in a ride. Extending his strong arm toward me, he helped me into the boat. I had no doubt that relief swept through the crowd, as I tossed my stuff into the boat and climbed aboard to safety. For an instant, I thought I heard an audible group sigh drift toward us on the wind.

Looking back on the event from the vantage point of nearly four decades, I can't help but see this as a metaphor. We have a Father in heaven watching over us while the tides of troubled waters overtake us. Even though we may have faith that His eyes are upon us, knowing He will take care of us, the world curses the one that left us stranded and escalates itself into a frenzy of distress at our situation. Finally, when God does come alongside and pulls us into safety, the world views His extended arm as though it was a random unplanned event. Mysteriously, the world never understands that we're safely within a Father's watchful eye. We simply need to trust in Him.

CHAPTER FOUR

Loyalties and Companionship

In early 1971, I moved into my own apartment. About the same time, I started a Boy Scout troop in an area between the municipalities of Lake Oswego, Portland, and Beaverton, each in a different county in Oregon. The First Evangelical Free Church, located a stone's throw from where these three counties meet, sponsored the troop.

Scouting offers outdoor adventures that appeal to a boy's spirit. I knew much of outdoor woods lore. Despite my wheelchair, I knew I might be able to offer boys a special quality of adventure and the will to seize what life might offer them.

That their Scoutmaster was in a wheelchair set us apart from the very beginning. Sensing this, they worked extra hard to make a name for themselves. Troop 25 was a maverick in the Pacific Area Council and the Barlow District.

We spent many hours outdoors, as those young guys experienced the grand adventures of boyhood, honing their scouting skills. When the boys from Troop 25 emerged from obscurity to win first place at the annual Council Scout Jamboree, all eyes were on them. More awards brought greater attention. The *Oregon Journal* picked up the story in the February 1, 1972 evening newspaper. At summer camp in 1973, they not only took first prize, but also broke the camp record with the best score for that summer. I worked hard to instill values from the Scout Law into the lives of these boys.

My own life took on new meaning, as I coached these boys to: 'Watch out for the weakest member' and 'Never tolerate a bully.' In protracted measures, they learned by experience and observation the value of being trustworthy and loyal to friends, family, and country. Ascending toward manhood, they gradually learned a man's behavior is at the heart of his honor.

Campouts presented me with the greatest personal challenges. We went out, rain or shine. The boys, in their youthful innocence, didn't see my chair as a problem like many adults do. Actually, for the most part they saw the chair as a toy. This was both good and bad. Surely, they didn't clip my wings by helping me. (I detested this in people who couldn't see past my wheelchair.) On the other hand, there were few obstacles they viewed as insurmountable. While I was making every effort to consciously stretch my limits, fifteen helpers unconsciously put my desires into action. The result ran roughshod over my limits.

I began to realize that a wheelchair could rock up on one wheel in hot pursuit of several boys while careening down a mountain trail and then recover without a wreck. I learned that my chair jumped logs, crossed creeks, and presented a rather intimidating vehicle bearing down on someone. On ice, it slid sideways. Other times, I found I could outrun a boy. Pursuing these discoveries, I proved it was possible to survive being tossed, thrown, and rolled, or just plain tumbled from my chair without being killed. This was all on top of the deliberate evacuations I made from it.

Early on, the boys developed a troop song to the tune of "Garryowen." It was the regimental song of George Armstrong Custer's

7th Cavalry. The words were different from the traditional lyrics of "Garryowen" and went something like this:

> *We'll work all day and march all night,*
> *And where 'er we meet we'll stop and fight,*
> *Where 'er we go they'll know the name,*
> *Of Troop 25 in glory.*

Although it was a bit militant, they began singing the song in troop parades. Whenever they marched in order, shoulders back, their patriotism swelled as did their chests.

The troop compelled every new boy to learn the troop song. It was not only a matter of pride, but also the dignity of being associated with a valiant cavalry regiment. It amused me to watch them march with a pugnacious swagger, belting out their own version of "Garryowen." These kids bonded like only boys can do in scouting, and I bonded to them. I knew I was good for them, but as time passed, I could see they really helped me put my life back together.

That same year I bought a black and white puppy from some folks farming along the remote Oregon Coast Range. It was part Border Collie, but the father was anyone's guess. As the pup grew, I was convinced this pup's mother had become more than casually acquainted with the local coyotes in that area. I named the pup Bear, because of her long, straight, black hair. Fully grown, she was a mid-sized dog. With long ears that stuck straight up, she was crafty like a coyote and as smart as a Border Collie. The combination was both an asset and a challenge. Bear was extraordinarily smart. Solely devoted to me, we shared a mutual companionship traveling everywhere together. Even after all these years, I still retain fond memories of her faithfulness, loyalty, and devotion.

She would romp with the boys of Troop 25 all day on outings. As hard as they tried, they could not exhaust her. They would hand her anything from a glove to a small pack and tell her, "Go take it to Dave." Off she'd go inflated with the importance of her mission, searching for me until she delivered the goods. On other occasions, they'd tell her, "Go get some firewood." Soon she returned bright eyed with a large branch in tow for the fire. Then she waited for her favorite words, "Good dog!" followed by the rewarding ruff around her ears.

I taught Bear more than any other dog I've owned since. As time went on, she displayed increasing willingness to learn whatever I wanted from her. She loved to retrieve sticks. When I threw a stick into the water she'd swim out grab it and bring it back. Of course, she then shook water all over me. So, I began teaching her to halt at the water's edge before bringing me the stick. Anticipating her instinctive reaction, I commanded her to shake. She caught onto that command quickly. If I told her to halt, she'd wait to shake. Eventually she obeyed my command to shake even when she stood bone dry.

Occasionally, a new Scout threw a stick in the water for her to retrieve. I'd devilishly tell her to halt, as she returned to him. Bright eyed, she knew what was coming. As he turned looking at me perplexed, I'd say, "Shake!" She then soaked him, reveling in the fun of a new boy dancing about shouting while trying to jump clear.

I also taught her to stay wherever I told her to lie down. She wouldn't move until I told her she could. Once, I told her to stay, and then became distracted and walked off. After half an hour, I wondered where she was. Remembering I'd told her to stay put, I returned to the spot. She was exactly where I told her to lie down. When I returned, she looked at me as if to say, 'What was that all about?'

Bear was one good dog. She helped me tremendously during my early years of healing—physically as well as mentally. I received great satisfaction working her into a remarkable dog. Her dedication made me realize how much she accepted me for the man I'd become. To her, the wheelchair didn't matter. She was my best friend.

Sue and I were still very much in love with each other. Despite my condition, we stayed very committed during the years after my accident. The first time I ever saw her, I was perhaps thirteen years old. I thought she was the prettiest girl, but I thought she wouldn't give me a second look. Typical of so many boys my age at the time, girls were a magnificent mystery. Sue, in particular, left me feeling awkward and tongue-tied. Finally, after a year, I gathered up the courage to talk with her. We immediately struck up a fast friendship that lasted beyond the next four years.

Sue had an infectious laugh, and she had deep feelings about life. Her favorite song was "Honey" by Bobby Goldsboro. Whenever it played on the radio, she cried. She would teasingly hit me when I laughed at her about it. As a young man, I didn't understand her deep feelings the song evoked. Perhaps it stirred memories of how close I came to dying. Throughout my recovery, she encouraged me to mend and get on with my life. I was blessed by her willingness to look beyond my wheelchair and see the emerging man. I deeply loved her for that.

In February of 1969, Dwight, a friend of mine, asked me if Sue and I would like to go out on a double date with him and a young woman he had recently met. After visiting with Sue about it, I brought her to my house. When Dwight swung by, the three of us went to pick up his date. His date was a student in her senior year of nursing school at Emanuel

Hospital. That night, although it took me several years to discover it, I met the woman with whom I would spend the rest of my life. Barbi was attractive, had beautiful red hair, was fashionably dressed, and walked with purpose that spoke of her self-determination. She didn't give me a second's notice, nor did I give her more than a passing thought. But I remember how well she expressed herself in conversation that night and thought to myself, *here is a woman who not only looks good, but is also a well-educated professional.*

Over the next four years, we seemed to live parallel lives. For a short while, the four of us would go out to various places together. After I graduated from high school, I wanted to marry Sue, but she was wise in wanting to wait and go on to college. Sue lived as a devout Christian, rock solid in her values.

I, on the other hand, was still trying to find my way through life without God. I really struggled with the prospect of not continuing on into an adult life with Sue by my side. The outlook of her leaving for college left me feeling empty. The threat of putting my life on hold for four more years overwhelmed me. My life had been on hold since the accident in 1968. Although that was only two years earlier, I was restless for more adventure. At eighteen, two years had been a long time.

Confused and nowhere close to reconciling my crippled condition, I searched for an active life. Perceiving four more years on hold without hearing Sue's infectious laugh was an interminable length of time for me as a young man. I felt trapped, as though she was trying to control my life. I took Sue's desire to attend college as a rejection. With mixed feelings of hurt, aimlessness, and a desire to honor her choice, I reluctantly broke up our relationship. Amidst all those feelings and more was a judicious sense that she would probably have a better life marrying a man who shared her values and was not crippled.

As I grew more accustomed to a wheelchair, I wandered farther away from home. Among my greatest joys was to spend as much time as possible outdoors. With a small haversack, a rifle, axe, knife, and a couple of blankets, I was ready to strike off to places unknown. I remember camping out with my brother Jerry one particularly cold night along a creek called Blue Run in Oregon. The night was threatening to snow. Having only two wool blankets and a bed tarp each, we built up a good fire. After cooking supper and brewing a pot of coffee, we settled in for the night. Sleeping in the open with heaven overhead for a ceiling satisfied me. The cold seeped into the blankets that night, as I lay there drifting off to sleep. Sometime during the night, however, I woke and felt rather warm. In the morning, I discovered the reason for the warmth; a thick blanket of snow covered my bed tarp. It had actually provided insulation from the wind and kept me quite comfortable.

Not long after Sue and I went our separate ways, and while I was still living with my folks, I developed a full-blown decubiti ulcer on my ischial spine. The sore was deep, and the skin over that vicinity swelled to the size of a small cantaloupe. Still weakened by my traumatic injuries in 1968, the combined duties of my job with the BLM, and my penchant to wander had overextended my limits. This brought me to the depths of despair.

I tried so hard to be really careful not to go beyond my limits, holding back from doing the activities others my age were enjoying. Occasionally, friends dropped by the house, asking me to go out with them, and I'd dolefully decline. It was extremely tough watching them go to the beach, water ski, hike in the mountains, and then go out in the evenings. I worked hard to take care of myself. Then this sore blew up in just two days, and in the morning, I was bedridden. It was the nadir of the emotional trials I faced. I didn't have any more resolve left. For interminable hours, I lay in bed. It was my only option to allow my skin to heal. Days ran into weeks, while again my crippled body trapped me, leaving me helpless to do anything more than languish in bed.

The sun's diffused light shining into my room rose in the mornings and fell at nights. I lay there in endless anguish, marking the passage of each new day. My struggle with the *visible* conditions I faced was one thing. However, I was not prepared to guard against the possibility of being ambushed every night and every day by the unexpected betrayal of my own body.

Furthermore, breaking my longtime relationship with Sue a month earlier still weighed heavy on my mind. Wrestling with that decision tore me up emotionally and left me with a void in my life. Without the relationship I shared with her, my life felt cast adrift without an anchor. That, combined with the loss of my legs, and then suddenly being ambushed by my own body was more than my heart and mind could confront at eighteen.

I looked at the clock, its second hand ticking unmercifully slow. My penchant for freedom was under siege by an undependable body. Chaos reigned within me, leaving me empty. My spirit was broken.

Trying to reconcile the trauma of the accident brought me one emotional bankruptcy after another. I didn't believe there was any real future for me. One day when no one else was at home, I gingerly rolled into my chair and slipped across the room to the closet. A thick cloud cover outside had darkened the room, promising a glum, drizzly day. Seizing my revolver, I returned to bed. I began slowly turning the gun in my hands, feeling its cold smooth surface. I stared at it. Deciding to bring an end to the distressing battle ravaging my soul, I pointed it at my left temple, holding for a long moment. Then slowly I brought it down. Hesitating, I stared at it for another period of time. Questions raged within me. Was it really a miracle that I lived in 1968? If it was in truth a miracle, I wondered why. This time, the question echoed not from a canyon darkened by time and laced by snow, but from a hollow empty room. In the depths of despair, my soul cried out in anguish '*WHY?*'

Slowly an answer began to form in my mind from an inexplicable source. Maybe it was because I really did have a purpose in life other than selfishly living for my own enjoyment. For the life of me, however, I couldn't fathom what it might be, but an unusual peace swept over me. In that moment I believed that these troubles would pass, and somehow things in my life were going to be set right.

Through the window, a ray of sunlight spontaneously pierced the curtain. Dad's wisdom came back to me, "When you get knocked down, get up, brush yourself off, and move on with your life." Then Mom's words came, as a gentle breeze blew in the window. "Your life is not yours. God has a plan for you."

The codes of my childhood suddenly emblazoned their truth in my mind, no longer as a boy, but as a man. Somehow I believed that God, whoever He was, wanted me to live. Finally believing that my life might have a greater purpose than my personal adventures, I found a ray of hope. The choice lay in my hands. The immensity of the option to end my life overwhelmed me. My eyes began to travel the length of my room. The breeze stirred the curtain, blowing the stale air away. Piercing sunlight brightened a patch on the wall and trailed across the bed. It felt good, and I yearned to be outdoors. Suddenly I felt released from the black prison of helplessness and woe that had been holding me bondage. A new presence surged into my body, encouraging me toward a new level of endurance and manhood. No matter how bad this ordeal beat me down, I realized an unknown God, whom I couldn't comprehend, could pull me through. This was a turning point on my life's road. I replaced the revolver with a new resolve. I have never thought about ending my life since then.

This brought me to one of life's basic lessons. I discovered that at the core of living, all humans are universally unprepared for ruinous setbacks. No one is prepared for unexpected devastation. The point is not *that* we react to the unexpected. Animals react to the unexpected. It's a matter of *how* and *why* we react that makes the difference and distinguishes humans from animals.

Most of us have been faced with a situation and then later thought, 'I could have done this' or 'I should have said that.' That is precisely what I mean. It is not the common experiences in life, as we ordinarily expect them to occur, that give us significance. It's the unexpected and how we handle it. This not only makes the difference in our lives, but also affects the lives around us. In that, our passage on this earth is not just for our sake, rather it's also for the sake of those we influence. As John Donne wrote, '*No man is an island, entire of itself.*'

The struggle I faced was still very much an uphill battle. My skin began to heal steadily, and within a couple more weeks, I was able to be up and around: at first for an hour and then two. There were some setbacks when inflammation flared up again, but I was set on taking whatever time I needed to recover fully.

After weeks, I finally returned to work and my daily routine, which I learned to appreciate better. Although my weakened health restricted me from pushing my limits, I had escaped the confinement of four walls. Even though I tried to minimize the source of power that changed the course of my life on that dark and gloomy day, my outlook on life had changed.

Once recovered, my jaunts from the city led me farther into the Oregon desert. Wide open spaces where I could see for miles captivated my interest. The silence on the desert filled me with awe, and I marveled at its beauty. When I would weary of bouncing around, Barbi would once again cross my mind. I'd seek her out, describing to her with passion the places I'd visited. The thought of traveling to far-off places fascinated her. She loved to hear of my many adventures. Born to a suburban lifestyle, she knew very little of roughing it outdoors and hungered for more excitement.

We maintained no affair other than an extended friendship, but our trust toward each other grew with time. Slowly as the years went by, we began to share our sentiments toward life. We visited about dreams, goals, and aspirations. I admired her insights and sensitivity to people's feelings. Eventually she began to read me like a book. Even so, we kept our friendship clear and simple.

Later, she moved to the Oregon coast to work the night shift at a rural hospital in Lincoln City. I drove a hundred miles to see her and share my wanderings. When I arrived at her house one day, she was asleep. Expecting me that afternoon, she told me to knock on the door when I arrived, and she would get up for the day. This was my first experience with how hard she could sleep. I knocked on the door, but received no response. Several times I knocked on the door. Her car was in the driveway, so I knew she was home. I tried to open the door, but found it locked. Wandering around to the back where she was sleeping, I pounded on the outside bedroom wall. Silence. So, I did the only thing I though I had left to do. I walked back to the car and got my rifle. Outside her bedroom window, I discharged a round. That woke her up!

Her cosmopolitan life was such a contrast to mine that I didn't even imagine a romantic relationship with her. In fact she was so well behaved and mannered that sometimes it annoyed me. Also, she was very devoted to her Christian beliefs, to which I still had an aversion. Although I admired her, I once told my brother Jerry that I could never marry a woman like Barbi. Nevertheless, we continued to form a strong bond.

Then one day, she let her beautiful long red hair tumble over her shoulders and flow down her back. Sunshine played its rapture through those red waves in three-dimensional color. The sea breeze magically lifted, then dropped those waves of red hair in a spectral dance of mystery around her face. In a moment of radical amazement, her breathtaking beauty captivated me. Immediately awestruck, I suddenly saw a stunningly different, mysterious woman before me. Those discoveries rapidly disappeared, however, consumed by a desire to be free of my hurricane deck.

My thoughts were preoccupied by the simultaneous forces of a passion to wander and my enslavement to a body that imprisoned me. All through high school, I had plotted to live in Alaska. Suddenly, in 1973 my BLM office was closing its operations, and employees who were fortunate were being offered jobs throughout the West, including Alaska.

I felt that the winds of fate were in my favor, locking my destiny on the course of a long-planned ambition.

I was among the last to be offered a job in Alaska, the opportunity for the adventure of a lifetime. I was twenty-one, and despite being in a wheelchair, I knew I possessed the steel to make my mark in the North. However, I was discouraged strongly from accepting the job.

Conventional thought dictated that the last frontier was no place for a guy in a wheelchair. Alaska had been a state for only fifteen years. The naysayers clanged out warnings of peril that waited for me. I had submitted to conventional wisdom after high school. That wisdom, which kept me from pursuing a career in the earth sciences, was wrong, but I accepted it and let the matter go, assuming perhaps I *was* unfit. Examining my potential for college through the irresolute prism of the seventies' cultural attitude toward disabled people was confusing, as were many things. Yet one thing that wasn't confusing was the teachings of my youth. One of Dad's maxims echoed in my mind—*a faint heart never wins a fair lady*—stood prominent among them.

There were many disabled people in the Portland area. A cultural prejudice was beginning to mold public thought. This prejudice created enthusiasm to accommodate the disabled, but brought with it an entitlement philosophy. Building on that was an attitude that the disabled were entitled because they couldn't do anything for themselves. With entitlement came the question of who was responsible for taking care of those robbed by circumstances. Thus, many activists advocated government intervention.

All of this rhetoric was built on an assumption that *all* disabled people needed help. Granted, there were some that indeed did need help. But the stereotype placed *me* in this category, and I resented it. Rather than having people believe I was entitled and therefore needed help, I wanted them to raise their cultural lens from the disability to the person.

Now, I was suddenly being *offered* an opportunity that was a lifelong dream. It was also a chance to escape conventional ideologies and make a clean break. I would not give in to conventional wisdom this time and let Alaska slip by me.

I remember recently reading about a one-legged cowboy passing through the Upper Green River Valley in Wyoming. Riding into a ranch with his good side to the rancher, he asked for a job. After a short talk, he was hired. When the cowboy dismounted his horse, the rancher saw his leg was missing. "Hey, you don't have a leg!" he said.

The cowboy looked at him and replied, "Do you think you need to be telling me about my own business?" He turned out to be a good hand.

This was the defensive stance I was forced to maintain in Portland all the time. If my own body wasn't ambushing me, it was someone who saw only what I was missing.

People who experience crippling conditions have the same sense of dreams, aspirations, and dignity possessed by all human beings. While we appreciate compassionate understanding, most of us want to maintain our sense of dignity, and we resent others imposing *unwanted* help. Those offering it often become a nuisance and an insult. I began to realize that my wheelchair didn't handicap me nearly as much as the overreaction of some of the people who saw it.

Alaska might be a place too harsh for a guy in a wheelchair, I reasoned, but maybe the cultural lens of Alaskans was not tinted by socialistic ideals. Perhaps they still had the ability to look at me as a man. In that case, they would accept me for who I was and not for what they saw through a presupposed cultural stereotype. Consequently, there was hope that in the solitude of that far-removed boreal region, I might be set free from the emerging cultural prejudice that lumped anyone disabled into a budding term known as *handicapped.*

Intuitively, I heard the sirens of the North calling, '*Send me your strong and sane...Them I will take to my bosom them I will call my sons.*' This was more than an adventure. It was a calling. So with boundless optimism, I accepted the job, hoping I might become a son of the mysterious North and finally be treated like any man's equal.

One month before my departure to Alaska, I was flying high on a dream about to come true. There were still things I could accomplish and places I could go, even in a wheelchair. Armed with a sense of destiny, I drove up the Columbia River on a drizzly day to visit with my old friend. Marty, a year older than I, was a rawboned young man who cropped a thick red beard. His piercing blue eyes could fix a hard stare on a man through his ruddy complexion. Living in the logging community of Bingen, Washington, he worked in the woods, driving a logging truck. When younger, we ran a trap line together, spending many days hunting, fishing, or canoeing the rivers.

I arrived unexpectedly, finding him getting ready to go hunting. He asked if I wanted to go along. "Maybe you should wait until the weather clears up," I offered. This was his day off, however, and it offered the best opportunity he would have to hunt. Marty had just bought a 1959 Willy's Jeep two-wheel-drive pickup truck and was eager to see how it would perform. Since I had only a revolver, I wasn't prepared to go hunting. Besides I didn't want to buy a hunting license from the state of Washington. Since we hadn't seen each other for quite a while, he urged me to come along for the ride.

Wanting to catch up on what he was doing, as well as share news of my pending trip to Alaska, I easily agreed. There was a raw cold feel in the weather. Grabbing my coat, I tossed my daypack in the bed of the truck and climbed into the cab. Marty then tossed my chair in the back. He drove east and north into the mountains on a main gravel logging road. Then he cut back on a dirt feeder, traveling toward the northwest. Gradually we climbed higher into the mountains, and as we climbed, we drove into rainy weather. Leaving the dirt feeder road, we turned off onto a less traveled road.

Naturally we kept a wary eye on the weather. "Have you been into this country before?" I hesitantly asked.

"Yeah, I know this country, but I haven't driven this road before," he replied. "I just wanted to see where it goes."

Weather can change to snow fast in the Cascade Mountains in October. That's when the permanent snow pack begins to accumulate in the higher elevations. Often travelers are trapped in the mountains during the fall. Their poor judgment brings dire consequences.

Ascending farther into the mountains, we encountered mixed snow and rain. Soaking the road, it caused the wheels to slip and slide. The wind picked up, droning a muted wail over the ridges above us. The area, logged maybe twenty years earlier, didn't provide much cover for game to get out of the weather. Not finding any sign of game, we concluded they were bedded down to wait out the emerging storm, as it moved down the mountain.

The road narrowed and dropped off to the right in a gradual downward slope into a narrow notch cut through a small ridge. At one place, a log with its end sawn off, hung precariously from the top of the left cut bank. Suspended in thin air, it extended three quarters of the way across the road at about cab level. A previous driver, who probably created the deep ruts in the road had also cut the log, enabling him to pass through the notch. Disturbed from its unstable pose, it could easily slip across the road. Marty had to fight free of the ruts to avoid hitting the log, which had inched farther over the road since it had been sawn. This caused the tires to spin as the truck slid sideways, but going downhill it was no problem.

After that, we intuitively sensed it was a mistake turning down this road. Coming back out was not going to be a cakewalk. Suddenly the notch opened off to the left, revealing an old landing big enough to turn the truck around. Landings are large graded areas to the side of a road where logs or equipment might be stored during a logging operation. I raised my voice. "There!"

Marty saw it at the same time and jerked the steering wheel to the left. My head hit the roof of the truck, as we bounced up onto the landing. Immediately we knew our detour had been a mistake. The wheels spun, as Marty tried to escape back to the road, but mud sucked the rear wheels down to the bumper. Unfortunately, the pickup was still pointed down country, and we were badly stuck. Making a wild guess, we were perhaps ten to fifteen miles from pavement.

Grabbing my chair, Marty shoved it toward me, and I swung down into it. We surveyed the situation while Marty lit a smoke. He was uncomfortably quiet. It was then that I really took a hard look into the back of the pickup bed. It was empty except for my daypack.

"Well, let's get the jack and get us unstuck," I offered soberly, wondering where he stored it.

His solemn silence portended bad news. Interrupting the sound of steady raindrops, he spoke in a rasp voice, "I don't have a jack."

"Not even a little screw jack under the hood?" I rejoined immediately, trying to restrain the unease in my voice.

"I dunno."

I found it odd that he didn't know. In any case, we looked. There was no jack under the hood. *That's not like him,* I thought, *but it's not a fatal mistake.* Measuring options in my mind, I thought, *No problem. We can cut a tree down, use it as a lever and raise the back of the truck enough to build a solid base under the wheels.* "Okay, we can still do this," I countered aloud. "Let's get the axe and cut down a tree." Silence.

By now I was beginning to guess that Marty was way ahead of me in this problem-solving business. "There is no axe," he snapped back. The uneasy silence weighed heavy in the air.

That could be fatal. Larger raindrops danced a hollow tune on the hood and roof of the pickup. Throughout the forest, rain tapped its warning of impending winter on the vegetation, while the wind rustled through the treetops above us. The air felt a bit colder.

As his words took root, my mind raced, *What in the world were you thinking coming out here without an axe or a jack. Are you crazy!*

Marty must have seen it in my eyes. He broke the silence with an answer that begged to be put into words. Almost inaudibly he spoke, exhaling smoke from his lungs, "You see, I just bought this pickup yesterday and haven't put my things in it yet." Pulling off a soggy leather glove, I reached into my shirt pocket, fumbled with cold wet fingers for my cigarettes, and lit up a smoke.

The rain began to drip off the rim of my cowboy hat, running freely onto my coat. Across my shoulders, I could feel it seeping through my clothes. Little puddles were starting to form in the low places around us, and a trickle was running down the ruts in the road below. We paused, smoking in somber silence.

Slowly an idea formed in the back of one of our minds. Perhaps the previous owner left something under the seat that we might find useful. I don't remember who spoke it first, but we flung open both doors and began digging through rags and papers jammed under the seat. Beneath the seat we discovered an old, rusty and very dull hatchet! It's amazing how such a little thing could be regarded as a life-saving treasure. Leather that once adorned its handle long ago had disappeared, leaving a rusted metal shank.

Marty quickly vanished through the trees at the edge of the landing, and I could hear him chopping—really with a dull hatchet, it sounded more like he was pounding on a tree.

Meanwhile I searched for a fulcrum to rest a log on in order to make a lever. My gloves were saturated with mud and water. Mud embedded itself into my tire treads, making it difficult to move about.

Emerging from the forest, Marty came dragging a tree over thirty feet long. We wasted no time swamping the branches off the trunk. They'd come in handy later along with the top ten feet of the tree that was too springy to use as a lever. Afterward, we had a hefty pole about twenty feet long.

Jamming one end of the tree under the truck and resting it on a makeshift fulcrum made a satisfying lever. Reaching high overhead, we pulled it down to waist height, lifting the whole back of the truck off the ground. Since Marty could move around more freely in the mud, I raised up and draped my weight across the lever, completely leaving my chair. Precariously hung over the lever, I steadied it. The rain had saturated my hat, and I could feel water soaking into my hair and oozing down my neck until it reached my back and arms under my soggy clothes.

Quietly Marty worked, quickly backfilling the depressions left by the tires and then placing the discarded branches under the wheels. When we were satisfied, I swung down into a very wet wheelchair. It worked! The tires were at grade, and we had a clear path off the landing. The only remaining problem was that we were still pointing downhill, and the road still offered no place to turn around. Even if we could have turned the truck around, the mud would have prevented the truck from gaining the momentum we needed to climb back up the hill.

Marty jogged down the road, disappearing around a small bend. When he returned, he said, "The road peters out in a small grassy meadow just out of sight, about a quarter of a mile around the bend. The meadow is muddy, but well drained with a solid base."

We climbed in, and Marty plunged the truck off the landing, down into the road's ruts that had softened with the rain. Careening down the road, we drove across the meadow, turning sharply 180° at the far side. There we stopped, facing toward the hill. The vault of cloud cover was rising, but the rain persisted. It's a sorry state of affairs to huddle around a cigarette for warmth in the shelter of an unheated pickup cab.

We were perhaps a hundred yards from where the road entered the meadow. Flicking his cigarette butt out the window, Marty slipped the truck into gear and began to move forward, trying not to spin the tires. We knew this was probably our only chance. Neither of us was a praying man, yet experience since then has permitted me to realize a force greater than that old '59 Willy's engine propelled us along.

As we crossed the meadow, he accelerated as much as the slick mud allowed. By the time we met the road, we clipped along between 25 to 30 mph with mud flying off the wheels. The ruts immediately captured the tires. This was both good and bad. Although the ruts kept the truck from spinning off the road, we were losing speed. Bearing around a slight bend, we saw a log across the road.

Bouncing and careening along, Marty smashed the pedal to the floor, as he tried to jump out of the ruts to avoid the log. Any attempt to slow the truck would spell failure to crest the hill. "Don't slow down!" I hollered. He cranked the wheels hard to the left, as we passed through the road cut. He knew if we bounced out of the ruts, we'd careen off the cut bank opposite the log and divert back onto the road.

His reckless maneuvering didn't work. Under full throttle, the truck slammed into the last six inches of that log. The post that separated the windshield from the door on my side jarred the whole log off to one side. It left a muddy impression littered with bark on the windshield. Then it hit the side view mirror, smashing it through my open window and showering me with glass. Glancing back, I saw that we had dislodged that big log enough that it crashed down across the road, blocking it altogether. There would be no going back now.

With just enough speed left to reach the crest of the hill, Marty slid on top of the hill and stopped. Then we broke into a roar of laughter. Bound together in a muddy handshake, we thumped each other on the shoulders. We had faced an ostensibly insurmountable challenge and won!

While the rain pounded on the roof of the cab, we rehearsed the events of the past hour. Then, inspecting the truck, we discovered the only damage the pickup suffered was a broken side-view mirror. The windshield was completely intact! (I wish manufacturers made trucks like that today!) I brushed glass off myself for awhile but nothing more.

That night, a thick snow fell in the mountains, closing the country down to travel for the winter. We surely thought we were lucky. Looking back through the lens of time, though, I often sit and ponder. Was it luck or God's providence?

CHAPTER FIVE

The Spell of Alaska

Within a month's time, I was boarding a plane north. From my first arrival, the mystery of the North never ceased to stir my heart and fire my imagination. The summer's never-ending twenty-four-hour days, the stunted spruce trees of the boreal forest, and the winters where long shadows slanted at noon all caused me to soar in the freedom of that open wild land.

A friend of mine, Scott Smith, was also transferred to Alaska, when the BLM office in Portland shut its doors. We both had worked for the BLM's Cadastral Survey Division in Portland, where we shared breaks and lunches often. Short in stature, Scott wore a thick dark beard and had a mop of curly brown hair. He loved adventure. Through time, we became lifelong friends. A single dad, Scott and his daughter Sherry, who was five, had come by ship through the Inland Passage a few weeks earlier. From there, they drove to Alaska through the Yukon Territory. He arrived just ahead of me, located a tract of land south of Anchorage, and set a mobile home on it.

Upon arrival in Anchorage, I rented a room in the downtown area. When Scott and I finally connected, it was the first week of November, 1973. He loved the wildness of his new place. Describing the panorama of woodland muskeg with the wide open space around him, he asked, "Why don't you buy a trailer and join me?" The permanent winter snow pack had already begun to build. I knew I needed to do something fast because I didn't want to spend the winter in downtown Anchorage.

The next day, I drove south to check out Scott's new home, located on a reclaimed tract of ancient muskeg. Muskeg uplands are boggy areas within northern forests. Black spruce, birch, and alder occupy the slightly higher ground in mosaic patterns laced throughout the muskeg. The spruce looked like trees from a Dr. Seuss book. A ditch surrounding the reclaimed tract drained the land, making it habitable. Beyond the ditch, the shadowy haunts of muskeg formed a barrier. Located eight miles from downtown, the only drawback, as we were to find out later in the spring, was that the dirt road was not maintained.

The temperature was well below zero, as I surveyed this bleak windswept plot of ground for a potential home site. Other than Scott's mobile home, the nearest residence stood a hundred yards away. To me, it offered a perfect place to live. The next day, I purchased a 1973 New Moon mobile home for $10,000 and set it up next door to Scott. Although the ground was frozen, the snow pack hadn't yet accumulated to a significant depth, allowing me a little time to settle in for the winter.

Before I moved in, I needed to build a ramp. The front door was three feet off the ground. I calculated the slope of the ramp to allow for icy days. Outside the front door I planned a porch with a landing halfway down the ramp.

As I assembled building materials, good daylight lasted about four hours. Short days, combined with the sun's low position in the sky, kept the temperature cold. The warmest part of the days rose between -5° to -10°. The dark hours of the day dropped as low as -20°.

Scott and Bob Olendorf agreed to help. Saturday morning, we met about 8:30 while it was still dark. Bob, an old-time Alaskan, showed up with his tools and pushed to get moving. It had warmed up a bit to -15° when we started. The air outside was calm, making it easier to work. The rough and frozen ground immediately caused my small front wheels to catch every time I moved. So I lifted the front wheels off the ground, moving freely on the back two wheels. The first time I kicked the chair back on two wheels, Bob made a lunge toward it. Then, straightening up, he gave an approving smile, as I cat-walked my wheelchair on two wheels. He made no comment. I had become accustomed to people feeling awkward around me because of my condition and making some harebrained comment about the chair. Instead he resumed working as if the chair didn't exist. I appreciated that.

Bob had lived in Alaska for many years and was familiar with its harsh climate and short days. His old Alaskan nature, borne on the ability to meld with the elements, kept us on track. His quiet manner and easy smile reflected the Alaskan lifestyle I was rapidly coming to appreciate. The fifteen-odd years he had over me had taught him a few tricks about winter construction.

Nothing had prepared me for the difficulty I encountered sawing and nailing frozen lumber. Nails bent as though I was driving them into knots. We worked through the daylight hours and continued into the darkness of afternoon. As we worked, the temperature crept downward, close to -20°. With the project taking shape, we called it quits in pitch dark around 5:00 p.m.

The next day was a repeat of the day before, and I finally gained access to the front door. From there I could finish it on my own. That night, I slept in my new home. The railings were all that I needed. It seemed as though my hurricane deck could almost sense this. The next morning, it didn't miss the chance to take advantage of fresh ice, introducing me to the shortcut route off the porch. Installing the railings almost became a matter of self-defense. Even then, on more than one occasion, it caught me unprepared on that icy ramp. If I got into a hurry, it would sweep out from underneath me, dumping me in a heap. At the bottom of the ramp, my hurricane deck would turn to wait as if to say, 'gotcha that time!'

Near the end of November, the daytime temperatures were below zero. With the muskeg to my back and the nearest paved road a half-mile away, I began to feel at home. With the ramp completed, I settled in for my first Alaskan winter. Looking from the porch, the Chugach Mountains rose steeply beyond the spruce muskeg to the east. Darkness and cold pervaded the country. As the poet Robert Service phrased it, *the white land was locked tight as a drum.* The deep cold locked all seasonal scents in winter's vault, except for the sterile smell of snow and ice. On heavy cloudy days, darkness lingered with a foreboding sense, robbing us of even a glimpse of normal daylight.

As the winter stretched on, I became restless. Looking for a place to get away, I was struck one day with the idea that Campbell Creek might give me easy access toward the east out of Anchorage. Ice on Campbell Creek froze thick before the heavy snows and didn't present much danger of breaking beneath me. A few roads crossed it, and all I needed to do was find a place to access the creek. Gathering my daypack, Bear and I set out from a park on Lake Otis Road.

We hiked until the sounds of the city faded behind us. The tracks of rabbits and ptarmigan crisscrossing the snow made me wish I'd brought my rifle. I appreciated being alone. The lonesomeness in the backcountry is unlike loneliness in a city, where I felt trapped and squeezed. On that frozen watercourse, I was free to live and experience the chance of redeeming myself from the unexpected.

Very aware of the much higher risk of something catching me off guard or jeopardizing my well-being, I consciously chose danger over security. Danger provides a sense of exhilaration, which is otherwise restrained in the bondages of controlled environments. Many people today desire to live in a secure, comfortable world where the unexpected has been reduced to the predictable. However a nice, safe, predictable world offers little chance of adventure. I believe there is an inherent sense of adventure in the breast of many men. Being confined to a wheelchair didn't inhibit my dreams or strangle my sense of adventure. In situations of higher risks, the challenge to overcome the unexpected surges in me and makes me feel alive.

Taking a wheelchair up the meandering course of Campbell Creek carried its own risk. Lost in thought, I felt the ice suddenly crack under my back wheel. It was disorienting. Looking up, I grabbed for a tree branch extending over the creek. Instantly, there was another shattering retort and my back wheel dropped down through the ice, nearly pitching me from the chair. The branch I grasped bent but didn't break. Holding it like a safety rope, I hooked an arm around the handle of my chair and pulled to extract the wheel and slide my chair sideways.

Looking back at the hole in the ice, I recognized what happened. I laughed. It was one of nature's practical jokes. Between the first freeze in the fall and the second deeper freeze later on, the creek level had dropped. This left a hollow pocket of air between two layers of ice. My back tire had dropped through the thin upper fall ice into this empty void where the permanent winter ice below was frozen much thicker.

During this time, chronic pain continued to haunt my back and legs. Often it set my teeth on edge. I spent many nights sleeping on the floor in my living room because its hard surface relieved the pain. Bear was content with this arrangement, lying down beside me. To ease the pain, I'd take a drink of whiskey now and then. It seemed to give me some degree of relief.

Gradually, after the accident, strength in my left arm improved, although it was still visibly atrophied. Whenever I walked in town, I'd travel with my right side toward the street. Sidewalks slightly slope toward the street. This allowed me to work my stronger arm against the slant. Recurring UTI's continuously left me rundown. In any case, I continued to work, despite these things. Although I still hadn't recovered the weight I lost six years earlier, it held steady at one hundred twenty pounds. In spite of these things, I cautiously pressed my limits, exploring the vast areas beyond Anchorage.

While the winter was enchanting, the summer entranced me with the midnight sun. Leaving town on the weekends, I'd drive with no goal in mind. Since the nights didn't get dark, I ate when hungry and slept when tired. With no schedule, I lived for the moment.

An incredible episode occurred in 1974 not far from the Kashwitna River in the spring when moose begin to grow their antlers. Bear and I traveled north toward Mt. McKinley National Park (now Denali National Park) and pulled off the Parks Highway on a rarely used road to spend the night. I set up camp in a small clearing, cooked some supper, and sat on the ground, sipping coffee and playing my harmonica.

When darkness overtook us and the stars began to tumble out of hiding, I rolled into my bedroll, watching for the northern lights.

Gradually, I dozed off with Bear lying by my side. Sometime after midnight, Bear gave a low growl, and then the most heinous bloodcurdling sound I've ever heard in my life rent the silence of the night. It was the angry cry of a large animal under attack, not far south of my campsite.

My nerves tingled up my spine, snapping me from a dead sleep, as I shot up with my revolver cocked and pointing in the direction of the uproar. Ready to spring into action, I strained to see into the shadowy forest. Then the clamor of wolves growling and the snapping and thrashing around of something large dominated the night air. Again I heard that dreadful bawling, as it became a terrifying bellow of desperation. I looked at Bear in the dim light cast by the burning coals. Her hair horripilated from the top of her head to the end of her tail. I whispered a coarse command to stay, but I believe she didn't want any part of whatever was taking place out there in the dark. Within a quarter of a mile, it sounded like it was in my camp.

Vagrant light from the false dawn shed indigo blue through the forest. Again, there was that hideous sound. Building to a crescendo, it became a death scream erupting deep within the creature crashing around out there. Sitting on the ground, I became obsessed by the sound of its terrified attempts to escape. A strange primal desire raced through my veins, increasing with the anguished struggle against what the prey must have known was inevitable. Its thrashing sounds lessened as the gnashing and growling took on the sound of a confident kill. Eventually its death cry muted, as the growling and clamor of the wolves faded into a feeding frenzy. The thrill of the kill possessed me. Sitting spellbound, my eyes fixed in the direction where, for a moment, an ancient surge of bloodlust burst on the land.

Diminishing into the twilight hours, the snapping of brush and a sporadic growl continued. Stirred back to my immediate surroundings, I became aware of the night's cold settling into my clothing, so I threw wood on the fire. Bear never offered another sound, remaining plastered to the ground as if she would melt into it if possible. Her ears stood straight up, though. Sinking into my bedroll, I drew the blankets over me, alert to the smallest sound anywhere nearby. Eventually nothing stirred. Whatever had lurked in the darkness vanished in the silence of the night. Gradually I drifted into a restful sleep.

I never discovered what had been killed that night, but I've always suspected it was a moose. The next morning while breakfast cooked, I poked around as much as I could in a wheelchair. Again, my limitations, always a frustration, prevented me from simply walking through the woods to discover the whereabouts of the previous night's incident. Thick brush obscured it. Any visible clues to those terrifying sounds escaped me. I had been a rare spectator; I witnessed an ancient rite that has replayed itself a thousand times in many wild lands since the beginning of time. It's the kind of thing that can make a man feel small and insignificant, and yet at the same time feel part of some grand event being carried out on the immense stage of time.

Some folks later wondered why I didn't pack up and leave. Others have asked if it frightened me. I can't say it frightened me. I *was* armed and could protect myself. Besides, the wolves had found their prey. It quickened within me a primordial sense of danger, begging me to live on the razor's edge of life. In that I discovered a latent sense of adventure arising from the ashes of the life I knew before my injuries.

In the comforts of my contemporary surroundings today, I can't help but think of the far more dangerous forces that lurk in the spiritual world that surrounds all of us daily. The Bible instructs us to *"Be sober, be vigilant; because your adversary the devil, as a roaring lion, walketh about, seeking whom he may devour."* This is a far more threatening force than the nearby wolves that night, and yet so many people simply ignore this adversary every day without as much as even praying or seeking the sword of God's Word for protection.

During the end of May, Scott and I left for a long weekend canoe trip across a nameless lake where we camped on the other side. Scott's daughter Sherry accompanied us. She was a bright-eyed blonde, eager to join in her father's adventures. Calm water allowed us to make a quick trip across the lake. Near the shore, mosquitoes hovered over the glassy surface of the lake in a dense gray fog. Turning into the northeast section of the lake, we found a low spot to land the canoe. The evening sun cast long shadows onto the lake from the trees silhouetting its shoreline. Sloping gradually upward toward a flat, we discovered a dry grassy area suitable for camping. Although the days were growing longer, they were still chilly. Rays of sunlight poured into this grassy opening with welcome warmth. When we disembarked from the canoe, mosquitoes craving warm blood immediately targeted us. Quickly we built up a smoky fire to discourage our unwelcomed dinner guests.

Smoke is the best deterrent I've discovered to fight off summer bugs. Once I befriended Jake, a mild-mannered Eskimo. As we became friends, I imagined that after thousands of years in the Arctic, the Eskimos had probably discovered a much better deterrent for summer bugs than anything invented by modern civilization. Scheming one day I thought, *if I were armed with some powerful plant remedy to ward off bugs, I'd never be plagued by the pesky varmints again.* So, I asked him. "Jake, what do the Eskimos do to keep the bugs away?"

He looked at me for a long time to be sure I wasn't poking at him just a little. Seeing that I was serious, he quietly replied with a puzzled smile, "The Eskimos build a big smoke and stand downwind." Well, so much for arming myself with ancient remedies. In any case, Scott and I stirred up a *big* smoke and erected our kitchen area downwind.

We cooked meat and vegetable stew with a batch of biscuits in a Dutch oven. After supper, I played my harmonica, and we began to swap yarns as Sherry listened, quietly poking the fire with a stick. Late in the evening, Scott and Sherry turned into their blankets, while I continued to play melodies like "Shenandoah," "Down in the Valley," and other old familiar tunes that drifted into the dusk, called night, during the Alaskan summers. That afternoon I had placed my bedroll a short distance from the camp near an old game trail. Twilight stretched through the night, allowing a few stars to dimly penetrate the sky as I went off to bed.

In the early morning hours, I heard something snorting and blowing, as it moved through the saddle that sloped down toward me. Listening motionless, I wondered if it might come close enough for me to get a glimpse of it. I silenced Bear with a hand, signaling her to stay.

Approaching us, it occasionally stopped, listened, and tried to catch whatever scent was on the wind. Confident, I could tell I had its wind. It came closer, snorting and blowing and then stopping. This performance repeated itself several times until I could begin to feel its hoof beats through the ground where I lay. Nervous, I got to thinking, 'I'm sleeping close enough to this trail that it could step on me.' Suddenly, I threw back my bed tarp and saw a large moose momentarily paralyzed by movement mere yards away. It must have thought the ground exploded with banshees the way it reacted. Raising its front legs into the air, it turned on its back legs and shot straight up the hill without regard to what lay in its path, raising a horrible racket with its rapid escape. Lying there patting Bear, I told her, "Good dog," while chuckling softly as I drifted back to sleep.

The next day, Scott and Sherry went out on the lake, canoeing after breakfast. Needing some alone time, I stayed in camp. Sitting cross-legged on the ground, sipping coffee, I stared aimlessly across the lake. Sunlight filtered through the trees, lulling me into a trance with its warmth. My chair was off to the side, and Bear was sniffing the ground in a nearby grove of birch, searching for a squirrel.

Suddenly, from across the southeast section of the lake, I heard what sounded like a sonic boom. Pondering what a jet might be doing out in that direction, my eyes began to focus on a large wave sweeping across the entire length of the lake. I stared at it, perplexed. As it neared my side of the lake, I was shocked by its size and the speed it was coming at me. Nearing the shore, I realized there were actually two waves, both big enough to sweep over the shore past where I sat. Reaching for my chair to jump into it, the wave hit the shore at sonic speed seventy-five feet from me!

Expecting to be completely washed over, one of the most amazing things I've ever experienced in the wilds overwhelmed me. Without making as much as even a quiet splash on the shore, the muskeg assumed the shape of the shockwaves. Rather than water washing over me, the land rolled under the fire, camp and me. Halfway into the chair, I was thrown head over heels back to the ground, as these shockwaves shot beneath me, knocking the coffee pot into the fire on their way to the trees. The trees tossed violently, crisscrossing each other as if hit by a fierce wind.

Bear came running over with a stick in her mouth, wagging her tail and wanting to play as if to say, 'That was fun. Do it again!' Birds went screeching into the air, and dead debris from the trees rained on the ground around me. Swinging back around from my summersault, I threw a frantic glance to the south, wondering if nature would send me another roller coaster ride. Small waves lapped against the shore. As quick as it had happened, silence returned and bathed the landscape.

The fire hissed from the spilled coffee. I righted the pot, then jumped into my chair and ran down to the lake. It rippled as if a light wind blew across it, but the air was calm. The entire event took mere seconds. I felt disoriented, looking around. I spoke aloud, as if to assure myself, "It must have been an earthquake!" Searching the countryside, I saw no visible evidence that it had even happened, except for the steaming fire pit. I couldn't help but wonder how many strange and amazing events like this are missed by folks living in controlled environments.

When they returned, I asked Scott and Sherry if they noticed anything strange on the lake. Scott had recalled a couple of unusual waves in the middle of the lake. "They were no more than a few inches high," he said shrugging his shoulders. "I figured the wind blew them up from somewhere."

"But there's no wind," I said.

"Yeah, I wondered about that."

"There was an earthquake," I replied. He looked at me, as though I'd been into a bottle while they were gone. I tried explaining what had happened along the shore.

Skeptically he listened and then laughed. "I would have liked to have seen you take that tumble!"

My amazement at what had happened to me made it hard to find any humor in it. As this was one of the thousands of unnamed lakes in Alaska, I decided to name it Earthquake Lake.

Another trip in July of 1974 inspired me with the vastness of Alaska's frontier. While working for the BLM, I flew out toward the end of the Alaska Peninsula to the settlement of Cold Bay. The BLM flew all of its own aerial photography during those years, utilizing the Office of Air Services. Our plane was a twin engine Commander with an aerial camera in its belly. The Bureau had contracted with the Federal Aviation Administration to photograph the airstrips over a number of villages that year. We left Anchorage around 5:00 a.m. and flew through Lake Clark Pass. The beauty of the wilderness burst on me like a spark on warm gasoline, igniting that old yearning for Alaska that had first come in a childhood dream.

Four or five years after breaking my back, Dad and I were sitting in a tavern one evening, pondering life's merits. Experiencing low ebb in my life, I felt rather aimless. I had a good job with the BLM, a fine apartment, and a loyal dog, yet still felt unfulfilled in life. Dad looked at me and in a short sentence made a point that has guided me these thirty-five years since. "David, when you get to feeling like your life isn't going anywhere, just turn around and look at where you've been."

Flying through the Lake Clark country, his words came back to me. Crippled by a circumstance beyond my control, I could have been trapped in some metropolitan jungle living a humdrum existence. Yet flying over the heights of unnamed mountains, I was fulfilling a dream that had started in the fifth grade. Looking back I wondered how I managed to be flying down the Alaska Peninsula. There was enough of a mystic in me to recognize an unseen force orchestrating events beyond mere random circumstances.

Cresting a mountaintop, the landscape suddenly dropped more than a thousand feet below us. In the span of two seconds, we went from a hundred feet to over a thousand feet off the ground. The magnificent splendor of Alaska spread out before me, inviting me to fill my heart's desires, as the mountains rose and fell like waves undulating in a sea of granite below me.

Past Lake Iliamna we flew, drifting along like a slow-moving dream. Periodically we spotted native camps and villages—isolated points of humanity in this vast wilderness beyond the fringe of civilization. Salmon dried in the open sun on makeshift racks. In many respects, the old way of life for those natives continued. Yet their march toward progress differed little from the rest of mankind. Motor boats occasionally dotted the surface of the water.

Crossing an area that would one day become the Katmai National Park and Preserve, we gazed toward the Valley of Ten Thousand Smokes. The eruption of Novarupta in 1912 was the site of the the largest volcanic eruuption in the twentieth century, spreading ash as far as Puget Sound in Washington State. Ash encircled the globe in the stratosphere with fallout for months. After that explosion, the valley possessed thousands of fumaroles. From the air, it still looked like a moonscape, a silent witness to a power far greater than the hand of man.

Approaching the plains of the Alaska Peninsula, the vastness of that barren land swept out toward the boundless skies framed by eternity. This peninsula is known for the bad weather it spawns, but the weather was good for flying on this particular day. Mile after mile slipped past us, as we drifted along the coastal plains bordering the southern reach of the Bering Sea. We flew about a hundred feet off the deck, giving me a close look at the country below us.

Nearing Cold Bay, the winds picked up, forcing us to a higher altitude. A cloudbank appeared across the horizon, blanketing the Aleutian Chain that rolled into the eastern hemisphere. On the tarmac at Cold Bay, I fought the wind from blowing my chair away from the airplane before I could jump into it. After I settled into the chair, Glen and Scott ducked their heads down, leaned into the wind, and walked over to the terminal. As I rounded the plane to follow, the wind hit me in full force. It was all I could do to hold my chair. I screwed my hat down tight on my head, as the wind tore at my clothes. Taking a bearing on the terminal, I tucked my head straight down with my face in my lap, pushing with all my might on the wheels. I didn't dare look up, or the wind would steal my hat.

Crossing that distance of fifty yards in the relentless wind seemed daunting. To escape its ferocity, I needed to reach the leeward side of the building. My muscles ached, as I slowed to an imperceptible crawl. The wind howled through my clothes and deafened me with its harsh scream. Finally reaching a point where I wasn't able to move the chair another inch, I wondered how much farther I had to go. At the risk of losing my hat, I raised my head just enough to see the pavement in front of me. Rather than seeing the pavement, though, I saw that the footrest of my chair pressed against the side of a truck tire. Pushing blindly, I had drifted off course just slightly. Laughing at the obvious foolishness, my first thought was, *I hope nobody's watching.* Quickly working around the truck, I soon reached the terminal.

Although the Cold Bay terminal was an international airport, there wasn't much to it in 1974. It consisted of one very small building, operated by one man. A coffee pot on one side of the room had a sign dangling from its spigot that read, "Help yourself." Decorating the wall above it and looking queerly out of place were travel posters of Hawaii, Tahiti, Japan, and Australia. I saw that Scott and Glen each held a cup of coffee. They chuckled, nodding toward the attendant asleep behind the desk. One of them asked what took me so long.

Beating around the bush, I told them I had been checking out the lay of the land, relieved to know they hadn't been watching me. As I poured a cup of coffee, our conversation roused the attendant. He hadn't heard our small plane arrive above the howling wind, and so he woke with a start. A perplexed frown furrowed his forehead at the sight of three strangers, one of them in a wheelchair. He seemed like a guy completely content being alone all day and didn't offer much along the way of conversation.

Over at the hangar, we argued with another guy to sell us fuel. He complained he wasn't expecting us and couldn't sell fuel to anybody just dropping in from the sky. After a few terse words in private, Glen finally got the fuel, but not until we paid what amounted to extortion. Lifting off, we headed for King Salmon, landing for supper, before our last leg home. That was the longest day I think I ever spent in a small aircraft. We landed at Merrill Field about 8:30 that evening.

On another journey, we flew on a straight course across the Kenai Peninsula, bearing toward Mt. Iliamna. From miles away, I could see its surrounding snow slopes were darkened by a sinister looking ash for hundreds of feet in every direction. From the southeast flank of the mountain snaked a bizarre-looking red glacier. Glen said it was the Red Glacier. It was so covered with red ash and debris from Mt. Iliamna that vegetation was growing on its surface.

Crossing the Red Glacier, we flew directly below the summit of Mt. Iliamna, looking up at the fumaroles. They appeared menacing. I must admit, I was anxious to get past it.

Glen asked if I'd ever looked down the throat of a volcano. My first mistake that day was to reply, "No." Suddenly, he began to climb the plane upward and banked to the right, heading for the summit. Slipping over the mountain's crest, he tipped the wings perpendicular with the ground and flew a 360° circle around it. Horrified, I looked into the abysmal throat of my worst nightmare. I felt like we were circling above a maniac holding a shotgun at close range. At any moment, I imagined scud would blast out of the vent and knock us out of the sky. Spellbound, I gripped my camera on my lap, simultaneously entranced and horrified in equal measure. It was a rather hellish scene. I'm sure I could see into the bowels of the earth though that hole in the ground.

As we dropped back toward the Red Glacier, I expelled a sigh of relief, speculating to myself, *I think this bush pilot must be crazy.* Leveling out again, he looked at me clutching my camera and asked above the din of the engine, "Did you get lots of pictures?"

My mind still reeled from having my first real glimpse into the gates of hell. Absentmindedly I answered, "No." That was my second mistake of the day.

Before it even registered, we were once again climbing and banking to the right. I have heard it said that when a person goes through a petrifying experience a second time, it's not as bad. I can testify that that's true only if all imagination paralyzes the first time. The second circuitous jaunt completed, we leveled out again and earlier speculation became true knowledge. This bush pilot *was* crazy!

Later that summer in August, the BLM radio technician needed to fly to the top of Mt. Susitna to do some work on the Bureau's radio relay/receiver station. At the last minute, I was invited to come along. It was a cloudy day, nearing late afternoon, and I was getting ready to go home for the day. Although I didn't have a jacket, I sure wasn't going to say no. Lifting myself up onto the floor of the aircraft, I climbed into a seat while the technician stowed my chair. We departed from Campbell Field in a six-passenger helicopter.

Mt. Susitna, a prominent landmark from Anchorage, is about thirty miles to the northwest and rises over four thousand feet above the valley floor. It is often called the Sleeping Lady, for it looks like a woman reposed in sleep. Thankfully, there were no volcanoes near Mt. Susitna.

After a short flight, the helicopter pilot expertly landed the craft, despite the wind. As soon as the doors opened, I wished I'd worn a coat, like everyone else. The wind tore through my light cotton shirt. From the top of Mt. Susitna, Anchorage looked rather small and insignificant. A gravel runway scarred the top of the mountain on which its lonely occupants were some scattered low-growing vegetation and an isolated radio communication facility. A rocky veneer made it relatively easy to wander about in a wheelchair.

Screwing my hat down tight, I meandered back and forth the length of the runway along the crest of the mountain peering over both sides. On the slopes, my wheels skid across the gravel providing no grip against the gusting wind. Occasionally it blew under my chair, lifting and scooting me farther down the slope. To steady myself, I rocked back on two wheels where I had better control in preventing the wind from giving me a closer look at the bottom of the mountain. This was no place for a hurricane to erupt beneath my seat.

After awhile, someone rounded me up and said they were getting ready to leave. Extending my camera with one arm, while bracing my chair with the other, I asked him if he'd take my picture. Back in the helicopter, I suddenly realized how chilled I was.

I had looked at this mountain every day since I arrived in Anchorage, never dreaming of ever reaching its summit. Disembarked at Campbell Field, I turned back to look at the Sleeping Lady. Chilled to the bone and dazed from the cold, my perspective had somehow changed. People in wheelchairs simply don't summit road-less mountains. *Had I really been there?* Yes, unless my camera lied, I really had. Once again, I had that mystic sense of something bigger than me or the forces of nature involved in the events of my life.

The distance to Alaska from Oregon seemed to magnify the time separation from family. My sister's arrival that fall refreshed and blessed me. Lois came with the intention of visiting for only a month. We got along well together. A mere twenty months apart, we were very close during our childhood years.

Fall came early that year, and the leaves began to change, as the rainy season arrived. This didn't daunt us. I used to say, "Nobody called me sugar; I won't melt." For our last weekend together, we traveled to Hope, Alaska, an old mining town that had seen its heyday years before. South of Hope, we spent the night at a place I had named Spud Meadow.

Leaving the Hope area, we traveled on down the Kenai Peninsula to the area around Anchor Point for a couple days. Lois was enchanted by this raw, rugged land with its grandeur. She fell completely under its spell. She left for Oregon with the full intention of getting her affairs in order and returning for good during that winter. She has called Alaska her home ever since.

During those early years in Alaska, I experienced many struggles and frustrations adapting my condition to my lifestyle. It was difficult jumping my chair across small logs, forcing my way though brush, and crossing drainages. However, in a journal entry I made after a weekend trip in May of 1974, I commented with a note of surprise that I was thrown out of the chair only once all weekend. The year before, I had been ejected three or four times in the course of one weekend. Slowly I was adapting my chair to my way of life. When it wouldn't adapt, I learned to slip out of it, pull it over a log or under a fence, and continue on my way.

Yet, I still looked at a mountain soaring before me, and my soul yearned to gain its height. As a youngster, I loved to scramble up the steep face of a mountain that barely had enough cover on it to find a foothold. My heart would pound from the strain forced on my legs, as I mounted a non-stop assault to conquer a destination I fought to win.

Once, when I was twelve, I nearly reached the summit of Mt. St. Helens with three other friends. Another time, while working my way quietly up a steep draw, I came upon a rock ledge and met a buck silently moving down the draw. Neither of us knew of the other's presence until we met. In one startled second, I looked up, as the buck jumped directly over me from the ledge above and like a ghost disappeared below me as soundlessly as he had appeared. These linger in shaded memories.

Without the use of my legs, I carried an unfathomable yearning that could never be satiated. When I poked at it with words, I couldn't convey the dull ache that echoed in the abyss of my soul. I longed to be released of the chains of paraplegia. There were nameless mountains that I'd sit staring at, lost in my own thoughts. I often ached to be lost beneath the canopy of ancient forests. I longed to draw in a breath where the air is musky from the primordial decay of the woodland debris hidden beneath the moss and lichen of the forest's floor. These desires loomed before me, both simultaneously beckoning and mocking me.

My inability to use my legs to carry out a simple task increased the time it took to accomplish it. These annoyances, every now and then, triggered moments of intense exasperation and agonizing grief. The mental challenge to restrain my emotions and get a grip on my antagonism over these shortcomings was occasionally more intense than the physical trials I struggled to overcome. I constantly grappled between living in a paradoxical state of imprisonment and freedom at the same time.

As a young man, I knew that this was a battle I had to fight in my mind if I was to come out a winner in the end. I could hear Mom's words echo, "You do the best with what you've got and move on." And so I did. As I expanded my sojourns that year, I fell in step with the cadence of Alaska. I learned to obey a rhythm that was superior to that of my own. This I truly thought could be the god I yearned to know.

Nature's rhythm was not the only one I was learning. The hurricane deck to which I was forced to entrust my hindquarters had a rhythm of its own. Whenever I seemed to be in a hurry to get somewhere, it took the opportunity to teach me a lesson in physics. If a front wheel unexpectedly got hung up on the most inconspicuous object, the entire chair would be thrown off balance. Twisting to one side, it bucked me to the ground. Beyond the prospect of losing some precious skin, the chair would frequently attempt to fold itself up for storage on the way down. When folding my chair, I always removed my posterior first. However, when I fell and it began to fold, it was like jumping clear of a steel trap. When a wreck was eminent, I not only had to guard my nose from plowing dirt, but also make sure I escaped a rear action assault. This was often a most difficult maneuver.

Confounded at times by my chair, I gradually learned how to come into sync with it—most of the time—without a wreck. Even so, it confined me from reaching places I desired to explore. Therefore, I was always trying to discover new modes of travel to penetrate the backcountry—ways that didn't involve the hazardous use of my hurricane deck. Hiking into remote locations was generally beyond the limits of a wheelchair. They were unyielding and broke way too easily. Although I became well adept at splinting broken frames in the woods, it was an enormous inconvenience. Even though my chair was handicapped, I knew I was not. I wasn't ready to concede that accessing remote places was altogether beyond my limits. It was merely a matter of selecting the correct vehicle.

🏕️

As winter approached, I began to seriously consider snow machines as an alternate means of travel. I reckoned it was just a motorized platform with a seat. After assuring myself that the seat didn't fold like a steel trap, I could see that moving it through snow would be much easier than fighting a wheelchair.

That winter, Bob introduced me to snow machining. I soon found that this offered me a completely new freedom. The wheelchair would bog down in more than six or eight inches of snow. But this chair on a track and skis would go into the deep snow taking me far from civilization in the winter. It also went fast! Obviously not having the use of my legs forced me to balance using my hands and arms on the steering handles. Puttering around for awhile I got the feel for how it floated across the snow. As my confidence increased, I pushed the speed, testing its limits. In that, I became a little reckless.

On one occasion, the light of day was dying out by 2:00 p.m. It cast a flat light with few shadows. Building up speed across a flat stretch, I hit a rock just below the surface of the snow. The result was a sort of snow machine rodeo! Unexpectedly the ski ricocheted, launching the snow machine up on one ski, sending me into the air. While airborne, it commenced to evacuate the area beneath me. Useless legs made this a serious problem. To make matters worse, while rocketing toward the sky, my bootstrap caught on the sled's hood latch. Jerked to halt in mid-air, I slammed down hard, while being dragged through snow by the sled. My coat encircled my shoulders filling with snow tearing at my shirt. Fortunately, the sled began slowing down when I let go of the accelerator, effectively aided by a human snow anchor. Fighting to escape, I got a good washing before I broke free and slid to a stop, dazed. For a moment, a few constellations circled about my head. Snow stung my skin and left me breathless. Thrashing to get above the snow, I felt like I was drowning. When I reached daylight, I frantically brushed snow from my eyes, ears, and neck. The snow machine had slowed to a halt perhaps fifty feet away.

Bob pulled up alongside of me, aghast at my disheveled heap. I had snow packed in my coat and up my pants. I looked like a drunken snowman sprawled out in an arctic jail cell. Finally pulling myself together, I couldn't find any blood and all my parts still bent as nature intended. As my heartbeat slowed to a steady pace, a spark of humor ignited the moment. Burning off the panic, we started laughing. It might have knocked me senseless, but it didn't kill me!

David as a boy in canoe at confluence of the Columbia and Willamette Rivers

Heading west on U.S. 30 in 1952

David Harper on family camping trip at Timothy Lake, 1966

Barbi Harper

David and Barbi Harper's wedding reception at the Salty Dawg Saloon, 1975

David with his siblings: Jerry, Lois, and Keith, 1974

David after newly installing a set of hand controls in his car, circ. 1971

David Harper's favorite dog, Bear

David Harper on top of Sleeping Lady

CHAPTER SIX

A Good Trade for One Small Band of Gold

During those first couple of years in Alaska, as I gained more freedom in my chair, I still felt incomplete, hollow and empty inside. Fortified by the natural world, I enjoyed mysteries hidden from many people. My physical condition, which prevented my independence among people in the lower 48, didn't trap me as much in Alaska's culture. Alaskans seemed to be more accepting. Yet during the winter of 1974, I experienced the most restless time in my life. My thoughts kept drawing me to something exceeding my passion for untrammeled, lonely places. It excelled my lust for adventure. Ensconced in those thoughts was a woman with long, wavy red hair. Merely thinking of her beckoned me once again to share my heart and adventures with her and see the enthusiasm in her eyes.

Meanwhile, Barbi was experiencing difficult times of her own, resulting in some dramatic changes in her life. Among other things, her mother had passed away early that year. Major personal stress left her earnestly seeking a new life.

Try as I could, I wasn't able to put her out of my mind. At last, in desperation, after all arguments I could mount against it, I called her. She shared her struggles while I listened. My concern for her well-being grew, as her story unfolded. What's more, I sensed she was drawn to me in a different way. After calling her, I flew to Oregon during Christmas to pay her a visit. Upon first sight of her, I immediately saw the strain she was suffering.

By April, she was breaking old ties and needed someplace to start her life over again. To help her "get her head above water," so to say, I invited her to Alaska. Her enthusiasm and budding sense of adventure emerged full of life, as she contemplated leaving the Pacific Northwest.

Before her arrival in Anchorage, I located a small house for her across town from where I lived. She moved to Alaska in May of 1975 and landed a job. Things had changed in her. But, more than that, the way she looked at me was totally different. Although we'd known each other for five years, I hadn't seen this side of her smile and the embracing warmth she possessed.

She came into my heart like the morning dawn. I deeply enjoyed her company, the way she smiled, her innate sensitivity and compassion for folks who were sick or troubled. I began to catch sight of a deeper dimension of her. Barbi made kindness and caring an art.

She used to say laughingly, "I chased him 'til he caught me!" In the land of the midnight sun, we began courting each other. Barbi worked a rotating shift at Elmendorf Air Force Base Hospital. The job offered her one weekend a month off work. At first, it wasn't too demanding. However, due to unanticipated schedule interruptions, her work increased. Time between her free weekends stretched sometimes to every five weeks. Even so, we managed to find time to spend together. I showed her the city amenities, as we enjoyed going out to dinner or taking in a movie. We also visited untamed places in the nearby woodlands where we were completely alone.

The five years we'd previously known each other had been nothing like this. All the same, during those five previous years we developed a deep level of closeness. We didn't feel the need that many young people feel when they first fall in love to jockey our behavior to impress each other. We already knew each other as we really were.

Barbi was worn down from the stresses experienced before arriving in Alaska, undernourished and underweight. With her resilience at low ebb, she contracted a case of mono. Much to her credit, she kept her job at the hospital, though she took time off work as needed to recover.

During her free weekends, we'd head out of town where she found relaxation in the long Alaskan summer days. Summer passed, and she soon found herself bitten by the spell of Alaska.

When Lois arrived back in Alaska in January, she settled into a job at the White Spot Café and lived in my spare bedroom. Around the first of June, my brother Keith came up for a visit. At fourteen, the difference in our ages diminished, and we enjoyed doing things together. He planned to be in Alaska for only a short visit, so the four of us decided to take a long weekend trip to Tangle Lakes.

Alaska was a wild land even near the highways, and it was wise to keep a firearm close at hand. The potential encounter with a wild animal lingered along the fringes. Keith and I had made a few day trips after he arrived, and I loaned him a shotgun in case he ran into a situation that demanded its use. He was no stranger to firearms or camping beneath an open sky. Keith savvied camping in the rough, so he put things together while I ran into town.

Lois and Barbi were in charge of getting the grub box organized. Lois offered to buy the food supplies. (Later I considered that we might have given that decision a little more discussion.) Barbi convinced herself that the Harper clan knew what they were doing, so she deferred to Lois's decisions on what kinds of food to pack for each meal.

We packed up our gear, loaded the canoe on top of the car, and on a Thursday in the middle of June left to explore the Tangle Lakes area. Intriguing places caught our attention, demanding we stop and explore. Someone would go to the creek and fill the canteens, or run for some thick brush that offered some privacy. Keith in particular seemed to jump from the car and head out into the bush to poke around, wanting to see what lay beyond the trees. Each time I reminded him to take a firearm with him. Living in the metropolitan Portland area, however, he was having difficulty making the adjustment to how wild Alaska really was.

The Parks Highway had been completed recently. The entire country was still raw, untouched wilderness only scantily invaded by man's permanent imprints. It took us eleven hours to get to Tangle Lakes from Anchorage. Close to the lake, we encountered a snowdrift blocking our passage. Beyond the drift, however, we could see a suitable spot to camp, perhaps twenty-five yards away.

Furthermore, we were shocked to find the lake covered over with about a foot of rotten ice. The only open water rippled within shore leads ranging from five to fifty feet wide. Although still broad daylight, it was nearly midnight. We unloaded the car, carrying our gear across the snowdrift to the campsite. The snow had crystallized into little balls of ice about the size of shotgun pellets. Everyone struggled to walk through it. Since it was more difficult for me, I made only one round trip and then decided to stay at the car and unpack.

Lois, being in charge of food, began gathering the kitchen supplies together, and Barbi pitched in to help her. Soon they had supper cooking over a hot bed of coals. I was getting mighty hungry with visions of a meaty stew and wondered what they were cooking. Experience taught me, however, to keep out of the kitchen. Usually, the aroma of a hot meal wafted through the evening air, giving a hint of what we could expect. This time, there was just the troubling smell of wood smoke.

I dragged the canoe down to the lake, pulling it by a rope attached to the bow. Along the way, Keith stopped me, asking if we packed a shovel. Pointing to a collapsible army surplus shovel tucked away along side of the trunk, I left. As I resumed dragging the canoe, I heard a terrible racket and turned to see Keith shoveling the icy snow. The little shovel I showed him didn't suit his need, so he had appropriated a canoe paddle for the job. The crunching sound of ice crystals reverberated through the handle of the paddle. Seeing me stop and stare, he hollered over that he was making a pathway through the snowdrift.

Thick willows surrounded the lake. Focused on scouting a path to the lake, I quickly dismissed the racket. Reaching the lake, I startled a large cow moose in the willows about thirty feet from me. She was making fast tracks on a line tangent to Keith and the car. Keith, furiously plowing through the snow with his back to her, didn't see her. Racing out of the willow to alert Keith so he wouldn't miss it, I shouted, "Keith, behind you!" Lois and Barbi turned to see what I was hollering about.

Keith was completely focused on the snowdrift, making so much noise he hadn't heard the moose break out of the willows. Also, he had neglected once again to place a firearm within reach. He first thought that I was joking about an imaginary bear nearby. He quickly dismissed the seriousness in my voice since I'd been chiding him all day about arming himself. Casually, as only a fourteen-year-old can do, he leaned on the paddle and faced the direction I pointed. By then, the moose was coming on hard nearly twenty feet behind him. Up until then, Keith had never seen a moose. Still having the remnant thought of a bear in the back of his mind, all he saw when he turned was something big, brown, and ugly moving fast.

Everything after that was a blur. He instinctively pushed down on the paddle and pole vaulted into the remaining snowdrift in a wild effort to escape. On his way up, he got his legs cranking hard enough that when he hit the ground, he'd be sure he was making tracks for the girls, both of whom had a firearm. The only problem was that he slipped into high gear while he was still mid-air. Now, rotten crystallized snow is not something you begin moving out of in high gear. With the paddle still clutched in his hand, he completed his wild leap but landed, spinning out of control. Fumbling to plant the paddle again for another wild leap, his senses finally caught up with his legs, registering, *It's not a bear, boy! Calm down.*

He collapsed into a heap one giant step from where he started. I began to roar with laughter. Even the moose slowed for a double-take. Looking over to the girls, I saw they were giggling uncontrollably. While we were still laughing, Barbi and Lois measured Keith's giant step. It spanned twenty feet across undisturbed snow. Later while eating supper and teasing him unmercifully, I asked Keith if he actually saw the moose. Looking down, he shook his head, laughed at himself and replied, "I think I got a good look at its tail."

Supper was a different story, not quite so amusing. Lois was really immersed into eating healthy foods. Sunflower seeds, oats, granola, and other such…well, interesting foods were neatly packed in the grub box, unbeknown to Keith and me. While she recognized the importance of meat, I think she packed about two pounds of it to cover the five days we'd be gone. I don't remember any potatoes on that trip, so I suspect they must have been evil. We were polite and didn't say anything.

Barbi, on the other hand, was rather shocked when she and Lois were packing the food. She thought Lois packed what the Harpers normally ate, so she quietly went along with Lois's planning. I didn't realize this until later, however, with disastrous consequences. For the present time, I thought this was all part of *her* planning.

Over the next several days, mealtimes became an ordeal to endure. Thankfully coffee wasn't regarded as a vice, and I found myself brewing it stronger, diluting my food more with each swallow. After every meal, I grew a little hungrier. As kids, we were emphatically taught you don't complain about the food, so Keith and I silently endured our suffering.

We spent the next day at Tangle Lakes, following the open shore lead around the lake to reach the upper Tangle Lakes, to no avail. So on Saturday, we packed up our gear and headed south to Lake Louise via Paxton. When it came time to carry the grub box to the car, I noticed it was actually getting pretty light. Even so, I resisted the temptation to start digging around in it to see how much food was left. Actually, it's a good thing I did because I may have started crying.

The ice was gone off Lake Louise, and we set up a camp on a peninsula that had once been used by the military. A light breeze abated the mosquitoes. The lake water was so pure that the only thing we carried for drinking while canoeing was a dipper. Whenever we were thirsty, we'd drink from the lake.

The grub, on the other hand, was becoming very skinny, but we made do without complaint. Monday morning breakfast was the bottom of the barrel. Lois fixed a pot of oatmeal, with a can of cream corn, sunflower seeds, and granola all mixed together. There was no sugar or anything to mitigate the taste. It even gave strong coffee a peculiar taste. Lois tied into the pot of gruel like it was the best thing since sliced cheese. In retrospect, I caught a hint of hesitation in Barbi's eyes. My stomach was gnawing on my backbone, as Keith and I silently ate what we thought was a polite portion. Looking around for the dogs, I found them hiding under the car. Perhaps they were afraid of getting the leftovers. That breakfast was enough to give a hungry coyote the dry heaves. Though I wasn't about to complain, I'd had enough. I was hungrier than a woodpecker with a hangover. Spinning in my chair, I said to Keith, "Let's go for a ride in the canoe."

"Where we going?" he asked.

"Never mind," I brusquely retorted. Loading my chair in the canoe, I told the girls we'd be back in awhile.

Out on the lake, I told Keith that I knew of a place on the southeast side of the lake called the Evergreen Lodge. I was certain that they had some real food. Rattling in my pocket was a little less than ten dollars. I knew it could buy two meals.

In the lodge, we discovered we could order two hot roast beef sandwiches for only two dollars plus some change each. Slipping from my chair, I bellied up to the bar on a stool next to Keith. When they brought those plates of meat out we thought we'd hit a gold mine. I started salivating like a dog with a meaty bone. Wolfing it down, I looked in my wallet and saw that I had just enough to buy another round. When the waitress came up and asked if we wanted anything else, I asked Keith, "Can you eat another plateful?"

Enthusiastically he responded, "Yeah!"

"That hit the spot," I said, after the second round was nearly finished. I felt as though I might live another day. Reclining on the bar, I prepared to savor the last few bites. For the first time in five days, my stomach quit aching. I felt guilty leaving Barbi back at camp. That hesitant look she gave at breakfast flashed to my mind.

In the meantime, back at camp Barbi and Lois became concerned because we'd been gone for so long. Being familiar with the lake from an earlier trip, Barbi said she knew a road that meandered over to the southeast side of the lake. Perhaps, glassing the lake from that vantage point they might spot us.

They drove to the Evergreen Lodge and walked down to the lake, immediately spotting our canoe. Wondering where we might be, they came into the lodge, as we were finishing our last bites of food. We were busted right there on the spot. I didn't want the girls to feel bad that we didn't like their cooking, so I didn't know what to say.

Barbi broke the silence when she eagerly said, "That looks good. Can I have some?"

"Ah… well…we…ah…I don't have any more money," I garbled almost unintelligibly.

Her shoulders dropped, and she truly looked crestfallen. "Well, how'd you pay for that?" she quipped, pointing at our empty plates. Her mood suddenly clouded over, as she let me know she was really hungry. That's when I discovered that she really didn't have any input into the menu. She also had been eating the food politely without complaint. She simply thought that was how we ate while camping.

I began to wonder if there was a log outside big enough to crawl under and avoid the brewing storm. Honestly, I would have suggested we *all* go to the Evergreen had I known how hungry Barbi was getting. An unbearable silence ensued while she processed this information.

I thought this storm might pass like a local squall, despite the ugliness of it. Then the cat came out of the bag when Keith innocently mused, "We'd of had enough, if we hadn't actually eaten *two meals each.*" It was if a thundercloud had suddenly gathered over my bride-to-be, and lightning began to flash through her eyes aiming all of those bolts at me.

At that, they abruptly turned toward the car, letting the door slam behind them. Instantly we were relegated to a realm where scumbags are kings. Chasing them outside, I meekly offered, "I thought you were enjoying the food!" Excuses sounded like blubber, making matters worse. The canoe trip back to our camp was like paddling to our funeral, but at least we wouldn't die hungry.

The prolonged five-hour ride home was like a dirge. Fortunately, some trouble developed with the canoe rack on top of the car. It gave Keith and me a chance to get out of the vehicle and away from the silent heat inside the car. Under a strong headwind, the canoe kept slipping around on the roof, providing some distraction. Several times, we needed to get out and make some adjustments. Ultimately, concern over the canoe gave Barbi opportunity to focus on a different problem.

After a few days of good meals back home, Barbi actually saw the humor in the grub box situation that ended at Evergreen Lodge. Looking back, it's given substance to a comical memory.

In the early fall, Barbi's dad, Ben, came up to visit and see how she was doing. When the salmon started running up the rivers on the Kenai Peninsula, a bunch of us went down early one morning to go fishing. We stopped in Sterling for breakfast, and I ate two-and-a-half meals, splitting the last one with one of the guys in our party. As Barbi and her dad were walking out of the restaurant, he quietly came alongside her, whispering, "Don't ever marry that guy; you'll never keep him in groceries."

That year, I started an art and photograph business, calling it the House of the Rising Sun. My logo was a Native American standing on a mountaintop with outstretched arms toward the rising sun. In his hands, he held a medicine pipe. The art I sold provided a small income and allowed me to purchase some photo equipment. Whenever I engaged in painting a picture, I sequestered myself away for hours and sometimes days at a time.

Barbi's first love was nursing. She was completely committed to helping others and dedicated to her vocation. Because she was so dependable, her boss asked her to work more hours, and she felt obligated to comply. Between my job at the BLM, my art business, and Barbi's job, our time together was at a premium.

Barbi's work schedule became more intense leading into the fall, as people either didn't show up for work or had quit. It began to take its toll on her physically. Weakened moreover by the mono she had struggled to recover from, she contracted a cold.

We seemed to be spending less time together than either of us wanted. On one of our few evenings together, we ran into a wild argument. It was over something so inconsequential that neither of us can remember what it was about to this day. I kept thinking, *This is crazy, I don't want to do this!* Not knowing what else to say to break this vicious babble, I blurted out, "Well, if you feel that way, let's get married!" I knew it would break the argument, with her either slapping me and leaving, or being stunned into silence. Fortunately for me, it was the latter.

She exclaimed, "Really? Okay! When?"

Admittedly, my proposal was rather unceremonious. Today, however, we look back on the memory and chuckle. Her long weekend was scheduled for the last of October 1975, and we began to make our plans to be married in Homer, Alaska.

In the planning process, my future bride suggested reserving a hotel room. But being impetuous and fully charged with my own destiny, I didn't anticipate any problems getting a room. It was late in the fall season, and Homer rolled up the sidewalks after tourist season. Really though, I didn't want to pay the expensive long distance phone bill to Homer. So with an insouciant air, I told Barbi we would be able to get a hotel anywhere and not to worry about it.

Packing our good clothes and survival gear in the car, we headed off to Homer on Saturday. Back then, we had three dogs. Bear, the dog I had when I moved to Alaska, had been joined by Barbi's dog, Minnie, whom I called Dinky, the smallest of the three. She was an adorable little brown and white Sheltie that loved to please Barbi. Her only drawback was that she had an insatiable appetite. She stayed close by Barbi all the time. Kodiak was a Malamute–German Shepard cross that we were taking care of for Lois, who by then was on the North Slope of Alaska as a pipe insulator. Kodiak was the youngest and the biggest of the three. At the time, we had no one to care for the dogs. Therefore, we packed them into the car and off we went into our future together.

On arrival, we discovered that Homer was having a record low tide that weekend. Folks from hundreds of miles around journeyed to Homer and the surrounding areas to dig for clams while the tidal flats were exposed. The hotels were filled, except for one room in the first hotel we visited. They could have it ready on Sunday afternoon. This, of course, was *after* the wedding. In fact, after an exhaustive search, we discovered all the surrounding towns were flooded with people, and the hotels all booked solid through the weekend. My bride was in near shock. As tears welled up in her eyes, she mutely looked at me reproachfully. Her eyes said it all. "There is no *room* available!"

It was one of those moments when the past focused sharply, as I recalled her words, "Don't you think we should make a hotel reservation?" I was quickly developing the clear insight that this would become one of those unexpected occasions that would characterize the entire weekend. Desperately I went back and pressed the matter with the first hotel we visited. It was a two-story log hotel with an unpaved parking lot. They were very sympathetic toward our needs and were so kind. We finally persuaded the manager of the Heady Hotel to let us check into a room a little before noon on Sunday to get ready for our 3:00 p.m. wedding.

With that situation taken care of, we needed to solve the more consuming problem. Where were we going to sleep that night? The evening was upon us. Since we were prepared, I knew we wouldn't freeze all night. Trying to make the best of a bad situation, we headed into the mountains to look for a place to lay over until the next morning. The night was turning out clear and unusually cold for late October. The temperature might easily drop into the teens.

My survival gear always stayed in the vehicle. When we left home, the only gear I told Barbi she needed was a coat, hat, gloves, and winter boots. What I neglected to consider was emergency bedding for her. There are times that no matter how resourceful one might be, plans seem to disintegrate. On top of this, the bone-chilling night was bringing out the worst in Barbi's cold.

We found a nice little clearing in the trees a few miles out of town, where I built a fire and set a pot of coffee steeping. As I rolled out the bedroll, it looked awfully small. Perhaps the darkness was dwarfing it, I consoled myself. The stars began to burst out with crystal clarity while the temperature dropped fast.

"This is what we're going to do," I insisted. "You stay fully dressed, leave your coat on and crawl toward the inner fold of the bedding. I'll do the same on the outside, and have the dogs lie alongside me for warmth." It was getting colder and not the best time for a lengthy discussion.

Nevertheless, Barbi objected with deep concern, "But you'll be half outside the blankets."

"I'll be okay," I assured her.

There was a sheepskin on the seat of the car, and I retrieved it to cover my upper body, intending to press my feet and legs into the bedding. I was used to spending nights out with only a single wool blanket and bed tarp, sometimes during snowstorms. Concerned about her cold, I pressed Barbi's head down in the bedding. Later, she told me she was overheated most of the night. Miraculously, her head cold vanished by morning. Since then, she has always claimed that I suffocated it out of her that night.

As I swung to the ground, I burrowed into as much of the blankets as I could. The dogs were compliant, as they were able to gather warmth from me and whatever bedding they could wheedle from us. Resting my holstered revolver beside me, I felt assured that all seemed well. A bad state of affairs was rounding into an acceptable situation that wasn't life-threatening. For awhile, I quietly watched the stars twinkle, hoping to get a glimpse of the northern lights, and then slowly drifted off to sleep.

I've always slept lightly, more so when outdoors. Sometime into the night, my senses keened in on the low growl of the dogs. I snapped into full alert. Something or someone was close to us. My ears strained to hear what made the dogs uneasy. Lying motionless, I shushed the dogs. Whatever was out there, I didn't want to provoke it or cause it to vanish without discovering what it might be. I searched the edge of the clearing. Shapes began to focus in the available nightlight. By the way they moved, I concluded they were coyotes. Gripped by curiosity, they had crept up close to get a look at us.

For a few minutes, I lay perfectly still, wondering what to do next. I knew if I hollered at the coyotes, the dogs would be evoked into an attack. I had been in many situations throughout my life when wild animals crept up on me as I lay alone at night, or stumbled upon me in the dark unaware of my presence. Most of the time, it was interesting to watch them. However, sometimes things can become unpredictable, especially if dogs are around. Thinking this through, I knew I could scatter the coyotes by firing my .44 into the air. The dogs could then settle down, and I wouldn't be worrying about them chasing coyotes into the night. Slowly, I raised my pistol toward the sky, cocked it, and touched off a round.

The retort from my revolver shattered the silence of the night with a blast that would shame thunder. Fire shot ten inches from the barrel creating an amazing display in the dark. The coyotes ran, as though all hell bore down on them. The dogs bolted in the other direction. The part I didn't plug into the equation was Barbi. She hadn't awakened from the dogs' commotion. My bride came out of a dead sleep, going straight into the air as if she were attempting to decorate the stars.

It wasn't hard to call the dogs back, as they were used to firearms. On the other hand, Barbi was a little more energized. The mighty explosion that erupted the peace had been completely unexpected. After she had a few words with me that I won't go into, she sat there for the longest time, wide-eyed, trembling, and complaining of the ringing in her ears. She took a dim view of the fact that I was instantly able to appreciate humor in the whole affair. Working hard to suppress my laughter, I had to coax her back into the bedding, assuring her nothing else was going to happen. My words by then carried little assurance. So far, the weekend seemed rife with the unexpected. She did finally burrow in, more from the cold than my coaxing. As the dogs and I snored in blissful sleep, she wondered what adventures would be in her future.

The next morning opened into a crisp and clear day. I rose early, thawed some water over a fire, and made a pot of coffee. When Barbi woke up, she stood by the fire with a warm cup of coffee, taunting me about the previous night. She recalled lying there long after I resumed sleeping and seeing something fluttering overhead. Thinking about bats, she lay there worrying they might swoop down on her. Before long, we were both laughing and thinking how we would one day replay the night's events to our grandkids.

The Heady Hotel was a warm and friendly place with the traditional Alaskan hospitality that was often evident in the seventies. The hotel has since changed its name to the Heritage Hotel, but still has the same early Alaskan hospitality. They had just finished cleaning the room when we arrived and graciously allowed us to take up lodging. Very few facilities were adapted to wheelchairs in those earlier years, yet the room seemed fine to us. Showering and changing, we arrived at the courthouse with only minutes to spare.

The rest of the day went as planned. The wedding wasn't fancy. The Justice of the Peace gave us her blessing with a few eloquent yet profound words. Five minutes of commitment between two lovers would span the course of our lives and an entire continent. Too proud to be married sitting down, I braced my legs and used a walker to stand for the ceremony. Lois, snowbound in the Arctic, couldn't get a flight home. Our friends Scott and his new bride Chris joined us, though, with their kids Glen and Sherry. Bob and Dee drove down with another friend Dan, bringing a wedding cake with them. The lobby of the Heady Hotel provided a quiet place for an Alaskan-style reception. Toasting with silver challises, a gift from Scott and Chris, we enjoyed some wedding cake and then high-tailed it to the Salty Dawg Saloon to celebrate.

Located on the spit at Homer, the Salty Dawg Saloon was a small rustic building with a dirt floor. Upon entering this fusty establishment, we were given a bowl of peanuts in shells. Brusquely, we were told, "Throw the shells on the floor and don't make a mess on the table. It keeps the dust down." We sat at a table made from a thick slab of timber lined on two sides with crude wooden benches. It was wise not to slide on the benches to avoid implanting a wooden impression never forgotten. In this rugged setting, we enjoyed many more toasts to our good health and a long future, as I carved our names in the tabletop. After the party broke up, Barbi and I drove down to the beach to be alone.

On that lonely stretch of beach, the two of us took a stroll hand-in-hand. We were as engulfed in our love as we were by the post-territorial Alaska landscape. The sun was low over the southwest where Mt. St. Augustine poked its cratered peak above the horizon. Again the temperature was dropping. We stopped in a secluded place, where I built a fire in the sand. Warmed in each other's arms, and by the strength of our love borne out of deep friendship, we nestled in the sand, watching the sun set through the mouth of Kachemak Bay. Later Barbi wrote in our wedding album, *We shall not walk this way again—but yet we walk from day to day on the strength our love gives and the building stones of these memories.*

Returning to my mobile home, we settled in for the winter. It was a cold and snowy one, and we didn't get out much. Early in the winter, we took a few strolls up Campbell Creek on the ice. Barbi was fascinated by the northern winter, surging her with new life. Those were good times. I showed her different sets of animal tracks, and how to tell time by the sun. In the years that followed, I have taught her all I know of the outdoors, and she began the even greater task of teaching me the finer points of civilized life. My task was easy compared to hers.

CHAPTER SEVEN

Winter Nights Bring Strange Sights

To say that I was rough around the edges when we were married would have been an understatement. My greatest enjoyment came from being unfettered outdoors. The cycle of life with its plants, animals, soil, air, and water fascinated me. I enjoyed every aspect of the natural world. Believing that balancing my beliefs with life's natural cycles would bring me into harmony with the mind and force of the universe, I diligently studied these things. Since I believed ideal wisdom came from nature, I lived close to the earth.

I had been able to pursue Scouting as an avenue where I could teach this belief. In Oregon, I had discovered I could affect a positive influence on the lives of boys through its programs. After settling in Alaska, I naturally began to focus once again my thoughts in that direction. So the year before Barbi moved to Alaska, I approached the local Boy Scout Council about starting a Scout troop. When I met with the Scout executive, he described a local troop that languished near where I lived. Troop 217 was a challenge because it lacked adult leadership. As a result, it never followed through with troop activities. Soon the boys quit coming to the meetings.

Scouting placed a large emphasis on outdoor adventure. Because my life was centered on the outdoors, I took this troop over with the idea of building a strong outdoor emphasis in its programs. We organized campouts and fundraisers and began attending council events. As we did, some reliable men stepped forward and committed time toward a dynamic outdoor activity schedule. This included Scout-O-Ramas, summer camps, and fall Freeze-O-Rees.

The coldest nights I ever spent on the ground were at a Boy Scout Freeze-O-Ree on Fort Richardson in November of 1975. A Freeze-O-Ree was organized each year by the local district to bring Scouts together in troop-to-troop competition, testing their skills. In October, the ground froze, and the first real snow didn't come until early November. The days had been unusually cold with temperatures lingering near zero.

Starting the day after Thanksgiving, the Freeze-O-Ree came along with a deep cold snap. We had experienced a few cold snaps already that fall. This one, however, bore a deep winter resemblance with high temperatures during the day lingering below zero. To encourage the boys to challenge the rigors of Alaska's winters, the Scouting council had a patch each boy could earn called the 50 Below Zero patch. Scouts earned this patch when the total low temperatures on winter campouts during any one season added up to $-50°$. This campout would give them an edge on earning this patch.

The Scouts worked hard all year, improving their skills for this event. Geared up and excited, they were anxious to test their new skills against other troops in an Alaskan winter. With ten boys in our troop, we weren't large in number, but we made up for it with spirit. At last, patrols were assigned troop equipment and an inspection performed on individual packs.

As we arrived on the base, signs directed us into a low-lying wooded area. Remotely located, the wilderness setting stretched under a light blanket of snow. The only sign of civilization was the two-track road. Close to the middle of the area, a small lake, perhaps two thousand feet across, reached toward deep forest. Six inches of ice and wind-blown snow covered the lake. Troops were bivouacked around the lake, and their campfires were beginning to send small curls of smoke into the air. A low, smoky haze hung in the air among the treetops, an omen that cold temperatures had settled over the area.

We immediately discovered there was no high ground to escape the cold. Waving his arm in a wide sweep, an event leader barked, "You guys go camp over there in the eastern sector." Thankfully we moved into that sector, which lay away from the lake. We knew it'd be colder along the shoreline. All together there were about three hundred boys and adult leaders attending the Freeze-O-Ree.

The cold metal of my chair penetrated my coat, and a shiver went down my spine. We quickly cleared an area, establishing our camp in troop fashion with two patrol fires and one central troop fire. The noonday sun wasn't high off the horizon that time of year, and it was already beginning to settle into the afternoon sky. Eerie light with weird shadows pervaded the forest under the treetop haze. Beneath the haze, the bustling sounds of chopping wood and pickup trucks disturbed the silence of the woods. The long shadows, combined with the settling cold and the press of activities, inculcated an indelible image in my mind, as I gazed across the expanse. Everyone was making haste to set up camp before mid-afternoon darkness engulfed us. Finding a flat spot, I scraped the snow to ground level and spread my bedroll on the frozen ground.

Event competitions were scheduled to commence the next day, giving us time to prepare for a cold night. Temperatures throughout the night hung steady near -15° due to a light cloud cover. Sometime during the night, it snowed a couple of inches. The snow on my bedroll provided an extra layer of insulation, and I slept comfortably. In the early morning hours, the moon slipped from behind retreating clouds as the last snowflake fell silently to the ground. With the landscape exposed to a starlit sky, the temperatures dropped. Some mornings, it's difficult to quit the blankets. That was one of those mornings.

I recalled a time during my thirteenth or fourteenth year when Dad and I were archery hunting along the Ninilchick River near Tillamook Bay. We'd hunted all day with only one meal of cheese and crackers at midday. It poured off and on all day and drizzled in between. Working along the edge of a small meadow, every time we passed against brush, a torrent of water shed rivulets onto our waterproof outfits we called 'tin suits.' Cold and wet, the dampness settled into my bones. Down on our luck by late afternoon, Dad suggested I work my way around to the north and take a stand at the far east end of the meadow. He would follow in a short spell, perhaps driving some deer my way. When I reached the far end, I looked around for a place to take a stand. As I did, big snowflakes began to mix in the rain.

Just then, I spotted a large spruce tree with long sweeping branches. Under the tree I found fifty years of spruce needles below the perimeter of the branches. The needles sloped downward toward the trunk of that old tree like a funnel. An opening in the branches offered a perfect place for me to crawl in out of the weather. Lying down and facing outward, I had a view of the entire meadow. I was beat and ready to rest.

Entrenched in shelter away from the wind and snow-rain mix, the whole day suddenly improved. I twisted about until the spruce needles conformed to my body, and I discovered they were drier a few inches down. Comfortably stretched out under the tree, I began to scan the meadow. Evening was coming, and my eyes were heavy, as I watched for the slightest flicker of movement. Soon a big buck emerged through the mist, dancing before me while I lay under those sweeping branches. Smiling, it walked up and began tapping its antler on my cap. Astonished, I raised my head only to find Dad tapping the end of his bow against my hat. At some time I had dozed off, and darkness was closing in on us. Dad had a good evening hunt in trying to find me!

Now, ensconced in my warm blankets, with the moon shining down on the white snow, I fought the desire to doze off like I did hunting with Dad. We needed to get the boys roused for the morning. Mustering all my willpower to shake the cobwebs from my head, I tossed the bed tarp back, careful not to allow the snow to tumble inside. Legs still buried beneath the covers, I quickly dressed from the waist up, throwing on my coat. My eye caught the movement of a shadow on the edge of the trees, as a white snowshoe rabbit flicked its ears and watched me in the moonlight. Then I piled myself into my chair. It was as cold as a crowbar in January. Wasting no time, I finished dressing. The camp thermometer read -25°.

One of the boys started a campfire at his patrol site, and I moseyed over to see how he was doing. It was still a few hours before daylight would begin teasing us along the forested southern horizon. Another adult in our troop was up, and we started a fire in the troop fire pit. Over the fire, we brewed a pot of stout, black camp coffee. The best way to keep water from freezing during winter nights is to keep a water bottle inside of the bedroll. A small bottle of hot water will give extra warmth at night, and the body's temperature will keep it from freezing.

The boys ate breakfast and were cleaning up when two district coordinators came by to inspect our camp and issue the orders of the day. The black spruce were silhouetted against an indigo sky and highlighted by the morning's false dawn. Despite the cold, the boys were in high spirits. The coordinators were suitably impressed when they discovered we not only had eaten breakfast, but also had most of our camp in order. Many of the camps were just starting breakfast.

Warming by the fire, they told us where the event stations were located along the lakeshore and how the activities were to function. We offered them some hot coffee. Enjoying our camp's central fire, they didn't appear to be anxious to move into the sub-zero temperature. Finally, as light brightened in the southeastern sky, they announced, "We need to move on to the next troop. Good luck today, and, hey, thanks for the coffee!"

As a parting comment, one of them hollered back, "Say, by the way, all the troops are supposed to meet on the ice in the center of the lake to get final details on the activities." At that, he waved and disappeared into the morning's twilight.

After they left, I asked one of the men in our group, "What do you think of three hundred guys with their gear meeting in a concentrated spot in the middle of the lake?"

Throwing more wood on the fire, he shared, "Well, I've heard that four inches of ice will support a full-sized pickup truck."

I mulled over his response, lightheartedly adding, "I'd rather it be your truck than mine." Then I added, "It's still only November, and that many people will weigh far more than a pickup truck."

My comment hung in the air when the boys interrupted us ready for the competition. I wasn't reassured.

At the appointed time, more troops began to assemble around the lake on the ice. A gentleman climbed up on a large box stationed midway across the lake. Projecting his voice toward the shore through a megaphone, he announced, "Everyone move in closer." The mass of guys were excited and although they were keeping their voices to a respectfully low level, the gentleman on the box was having difficulty carrying his voice out to the crowd. Thus, he kept urging everyone to move in closer. The event coordinators were milling on the fringes, trying to gather the boys into a tighter circle.

Intuitively, holding back, I still pondered the physical strength of the ice holding that many people. No doubt sensing my reluctance, our troop lingered twenty feet from the shore. As the coordinators urged everyone out onto the lake, our boys started to move out slowly. Indecisive, my hands delayed mustering the necessary momentum to move forward. The boys cast me an inquisitive look, as they moved toward the lake's center, but, passing me, said nothing. Although adverse to starting an insurrection, I just didn't feel right. Watching the crowd gather in a tighter group, I finally reached a conclusion.

The boys were about fifty feet out from me when I suddenly shouted, "You guys come back here." A couple of the district Scout leaders cast me an annoyed look, and one objected. Across the expanse, I explained my concern. It was met with immediate disdain. The boys were perplexed. Until then, I hadn't shared my thoughts with them. Watching the other troops draw toward the center, my troop was confused. Feelings ran strong that they were doing something wrong, even though I explained what might happen. Stragglers passing by scoffed at me, while another urged the boys to close rank anyway. Firmly, I lowered my voice telling our boys, "Just hold your ground. We can hear okay from here."

Nothing gave any indication to confirm that my unease was valid. Scouts and leaders loosely concentrated toward the center of the frozen lake, making all my apprehension seem senseless. Those on the circle's fringe softly bantered among themselves, and the man on the box was still trying to speak over the clamor. In one final effort to be heard, he urged everyone in just a little closer. That was all it took.

In that still, cold morning air, it sounded like cannon fire. At the center of the crowd, water shot straight into the air maybe ten feet. I've never since witnessed such a mass evacuation of human beings in my life. It was as if a train whistle blew in the midst of a thousand rabbits. Within two seconds, the central part of the lake was clear of everything but some scattered gear and the kicked-over box upon which the announcer once stood.

Folks headed for all points of the compass simultaneously trying to outrun the cracks in the ice. Nobody fell through, but they obviously didn't want to wait and see what would happen next. Heroes were born that day, as some boys turned to encourage others. A few high-stepping adults revealed their true color, gaining the shore in leaps ahead of their boys. My boys, although they were only twenty feet from the shore, spared no time heading for terra firma.

Hesitating for a split second, I was seized by the comical exodus. Percolating water through the cracks made it so slick, people lost their footing, blundering and slipping to all fours in their chaotic attempt to escape. Water trickled through the ice wherever a crack appeared. However, the fleeing crowd relieved the pressure on the ice, resulting in less seepage. A fissure shooting across the ice toward me, followed by oozing water, finally motivated me into flight also.

Racing between my wheels, it spread a small puddle under me, making the ice surface suddenly too slick to escape. Frantically spinning my wheels and going nowhere, all I could think was, *this is not a good day to die.* Looking up to see if anyone risked venturing out to give me a hand, I saw my whole troop on high ground pointing fingers at me. By then everyone else knew the danger was past. Some were reeling on haunches laughing, while others stood looking agape in my direction. With my hands working at top speed and the chair not moving, the irony didn't escape me that among those three hundred people, I was the only one trapped on the ice! Someone finally stopped laughing enough to come slip-sliding out to give me a hand.

As fast as it started, it was over. Obviously, the ice was indeed too thick for any single person to fall through. It had just cracked under the massive weight, forcing the water to come through in the center like a geyser. At -20°, the water froze within minutes.

Order quickly prevailed over the chaos, as the announcer relocated to the shore. A rather subdued group reassembled in a wider concentric circle on the ice near the shore's edge. Everyone could hear the speaker quite clearly after that. What I think they were really intently listening for, though, was the slightest sound of cracking ice heralding an alarm to run! I know I don't remember a thing that guy had to say.

It's taken me many years since that day to see the parallel, but how many times do we follow the crowd, thinking that it can't be wrong when we have an inner voice saying, "Don't do that." We often face perils and encounter troubles just because we think the wisdom of man is greater than the One who speaks to our hearts. Even when we do heed that voice, how often do we stand just twenty feet from the rock of our salvation, allowing ourselves to be drawn to the crowd? Assuming our position is secure, we falsely assure ourselves that we are still separated from the crowd and beyond the danger of sin. Then when events don't go our way, we spin our wheels futilely, as we desperately try to escape, but have no power in our own strength. Elijah once cried out to Israel, *"How long will you hesitate between two opinions? If the Lord is God follow him."*

After the ice incident, the competition went as planned. Our boys even took home some ribbons to hang on their troop flag. Throughout the day, conversations relived the ice-breaking event of the day. I'd wager, anyone alive today that recalls the event has a good story to tell.

As the day wore on, the temperatures warmed, and the cold released its grip. Some of the boys searched the perimeters to bring in dead wood, heaping an enormous pile of branches near the fire. They were burning diamond willow. The price folks in the Pacific Northwest used to pay for a well-finished diamond willow walking stick floated through my mind. I shook my head, watching another stick go into the fire.

While the boys trickled into camp, one of the men in our troop stretched a rope between two trees, about eight feet off the ground. He tied a large space blanket from the rope to the ground at an angle. This formed a lean-to facing the fire. Several boys and this man stood comfortably within this makeshift arrangement.

The longer I sat still in one spot, the colder I became. I'd get one side warmed by the fire while my other side would be freezing. Soon someone said to me, "You ought to stand in front of this space blanket." Not having owned a space blanket, I viewed it as another gimmick to relieve the gullible of their money.

Everybody insisted it was really warm. Making room for me, I ventured to move within its shield. I was flabbergasted at the change in temperature. The space blanket radiated the heat back toward the fire and both sides of me became warm at the same time. In fact, I needed to move away because I was too warm. As we moved in and out from under that lean-to, we began to wonder how warm it really was. Out of the lean-to it was -15°. Someone hung a thermometer at the top of the lean-to. In five minutes, it registered 60°! To this day, I consider a space blanket one of the most critical pieces of equipment that everyone should have in their survival pack.

That night was considerably colder than the night before, but we fared through it without incident. After breakfast, however, I believe we burned every dry stick within a thousand yards of that Freeze-O-Ree site. Packing up our camp, we left by noon. Each boy walked a little taller as he left, confident in the victories he had gained over other troops and the forces of winter. After that, winter took on its cold gray mantle.

On occasion, as winter progressed, Barbi and I wandered into town and walked the mall or downtown area, taking in the amenities of the Alaskan culture. Anchorage was very different in the seventies. While it was in many respects an offshoot to Elmendorf AFB and Fort Richardson, whose personnel reflected the culture of the lower 48 states, it was also a regional hub of frontier activity and retained its frontier attitude. It serviced the vast number of villages throughout the Alaska Peninsula, interior, Cook Inlet, and southern coastal areas. This included the scattered rural people living on the frontier, comprised of homesteaders, miners, trappers, and traders who had settled those areas. Consequently, its merging frontier and military cultures stood in contrast, clearly making the town a novelty to visit.

My friend Jake and I were visiting one afternoon in the fourth floor office where we worked. The hubbub of the city rushed beneath us. Reminiscing of his home in the Arctic, he commented, "Dave, do you know what I like about Anchorage?"

Looking at him quizzically, I replied, "No, Jake, what?"

Staring out the window he whimsically replied, "It's close to Alaska." His answer was a simple reflection based on a genuine observation and not in the least bit critical. As I grew to know Jake even more, I grew to appreciate his bush wisdom.

Acknowledging my respect for his culture, he introduced me to the Eskimo ways. Among these were the foods that his relatives would send him from the bush. One of those delicacies was muktuk. Spelled a variety of different ways, muktuk is whale skin and blubber, usually eaten raw. When Jake first gave me a piece of it, I think he expected me to reject it. I will confess it was very different than anything I'd ever eaten before. I chewed it slowly and let the juices flow across my taste buds before I swallowed it.

"Do you like it?" he asked.

"Yes, it's different, but I do," I told him. Then I asked, "Do you have any more?"

His eyes became wide. For a moment he stared at me. Then he told me that I was the only white person he ever met that would eat muktuk. Lowering his voice he confided, "After I returned to my village from being away for four years at college, I had to reacquire a taste for my native diet."

Since I liked muktuk, every time his relatives sent him food from the village, he would share some of it with me.

That first winter after Barbi and I were married was a tough one. The chronic pain I suffered in my back injury increasingly plagued me. Pain could give me a short fuse, causing me to blow at minor annoyances. Whiskey continued to ease the intensity of it, and I found I was drinking more. I continued to crawl out of bed after two or three hours of sleep and take a drink. Then I'd wander about the house, stretching to escape the pain in my back while it took effect. At first, Barbi woke every time I slipped out of bed. She told me I had the sleeping habits of a coyote. Within a few months, however, she became used to it, not knowing when I would leave or return.

That Christmas was Barbi's first away from home and the second since her mother had passed away. As it approached, she was despondent, being away from friends and relatives. The cumulative affects of the previous twelve months in the lower 48 and the long winter nights took a deep toll on her. Trying to cheer her up, I wondered aloud how to celebrate Christmas. I didn't have a Christmas tree the year before, lacking inclination and decorations. Barbi didn't have any decorations either, but this was not going to daunt her. I suggested we didn't need a tree, but that was as blasphemous as letting a mouse loose in the middle of a church service. Pinching and saving in the weeks before Christmas, Barbi saved enough to buy some cranberries and extra sugar.

Searching for ways to decorate, I recalled a Christmas years before when I was about nine years old. Times were tough for my folks. Dad worked long hard hours. With Christmas coming, we had no prospects for a Christmas tree that year. My brother Keith had been born the previous spring, rounding us out to four siblings. Mom's dad had passed away almost three years earlier. Events in her life had sent her into despair. She had been scrimping to buy a few things for Christmas and kept these things hidden from us kids, but a Christmas tree was not in the budget.

Not wanting to disappoint us, she found a huge tumbleweed and brought it into the house. This was to be our Christmas tree for the holiday. We kids sneered over this dusty old tumbleweed, but Mom had a way of encouraging us, even when she didn't feel up to it. Building a little stand for it and bundling us up, she took us outside. There she began to spray it with white flocking from a can. It seemed a bit silly to me, but between her enthusiasm and that can of flocking, I became infected with the spirit of this project.

"Do we have anything to hang on it?" we chortled.

"We'll see," she mused.

All the ornaments I knew we had were too big for it, even though it was two or three feet across.

Taking it into the house, she placed it in a prominent place before pulling out some little glass Christmas balls no bigger than marbles. They were wonderful. I'd never seen balls that size, and they fascinated me. We decorated that tumbleweed and transformed it into the most beautiful tree that I'd ever seen.

Later, on the eve of Christmas while Dad was still at work, my grandfather Pop brought in a real Christmas tree he'd gathered from somewhere. Mom was thrilled with it. Pulling out all the old familiar ornaments she busied herself with the tree. I stood back by the tumbleweed, however, and thought to myself, *that tree will never be as beautiful as our tumbleweed.*

Barbi and I went to the woods late one cold and frosty morning, as the sun was coming up, and cut down a little "Dr. Seuss" spruce tree. Onto this I built a wooden stand. We didn't have much, but her enthusiasm to decorate the tree was contagious. We strung cranberries and popcorn together and made candied ornaments with Christmas cookie cutters. Using crepe paper and aluminum foil, we made other ornaments and did our best to make it look like a beautiful and dignified tree. We didn't have any lights to hang on it so it didn't shine; yet it was a beautiful tree nevertheless. After New Year's Day, Barbi gently wrapped those ornaments that could be preserved in tissue paper and put them away for the next year.

We have celebrated many Christmases since that time, and we have had some really beautiful trees. But every year, there is a moment when we soberly and gently pull those few Christmas ornaments out of the box from 1975. Tenderly we unwrap them from the old worn tissue paper, and affectionately place them on our tree. In the solemnity of that moment, we each silently reflect on the joy of that first Christmas, the hard times we struggled through back then, and the love we shared.

In January, the temperatures were consistently below zero. The long winter nights and pervasive darkness tend to do strange things to the mind. We both became susceptible to the darkness one particularly cold winter's night by developing a sudden predilection for homemade ice cream. Furthermore, we discovered our ice trays were stored in the cupboard. (Back then, not many people took up freezer space to make ice cubes during January in Alaska.) Barbi immediately became discouraged. Where she came from, people had to get ice from a freezer. I couldn't help but laugh at the irony. There we were, during the dead of winter in the coldest state of the Union, discouraged over a lack of ice. Despondently she challenged, "What are you laughing at?"

Chuckling, I said, "Here we are surrounded by ice, and we're depressed because there's none in the freezer!" That made her laugh also.

Next was the matter of securing ice from under the snow. Campbell Creek swung south near Dimond Boulevard. Not far to the west of Arctic Boulevard, there was a spot where we could pull down to the creek. There wasn't a house anywhere nearby back then. So grabbing an axe, we bundled up about 10:00 p.m. and headed for the creek. Of course the creek was frozen quite solid. Finding a stress fracture in the ice, we began chunking away bits of ice out of the creek. All else lay in silence beyond the creek bed, frozen tight as rawhide. As we worked, I noticed the northern lights making faint streaks across a moonless sky.

We were working away in the headlights of our car, minding our own business. Steam from our breath hung in the air. As Barbi was filling the last of the ice into our gunnysack, a vehicle caught our attention, as it slowed on Dimond Boulevard. Turning in slowly alongside our car, it kept its lights shining on us.

We had been gone about forty-five minutes. The cold was seeping into our clothes, and we were ready to head back to the house. Neither of us felt much like visiting. The vehicle door gradually opened, and another bright beam of light flashed in my face as if four headlights were insufficient. Without identifying himself, a male voice demanded, "What are you two doing down there?"

When someone shines a flashlight in my face, I tend to believe they're doing it to get an upper hand. Since we were minding our own business and not bothering anyone else, I was not about to be intimidated. My hostility immediately rose. Still holding the axe, I demanded back at the faceless voice, "Who's asking!"

Repeating himself in a more bellicose voice, he replied, "I said, what are you doing down there!"

Telling Barbi to get behind me and holding my axe in a menacing way, I also raised my voice, once again retorting, "Who's asking!!" At this point, I felt like he was goading me into a battle, which I was all too willing to fight.

There was a long pause. Seconds ticked by as we squared off with one another, both standing our ground. Silence reclaimed the moment. Then, seeing this was going to a level no sane person would go at midnight in January, he silently turned the flashlight out of my face and onto his chest. While I was still blinded, he appeared as a mere silhouette behind two sets of headlights. I could clearly see the light reflect from the badge on his chest, though.

Annoyed, yet somewhat relieved, I lowered the axe to my lap and in a steely low voice said, "We're making ice cream." That sounded stupid, I thought. Then I followed in a calmer voice, "We need ice for the ice cream mill."

Incredulously, as if he didn't hear me right, he replied in an eased voice, "You're doing what?"

"We're getting ice," I replied. "We had a hankering for ice cream, and we needed ice."

Again there was a long period of silence. Having not moved and still standing on the ice, we were really getting cold. I couldn't figure out what kind of a fool's errand this guy thought he was taking on, disturbing our peaceful efforts to make ice cream. He must have been getting cold too. Slowly he turned to get back into his squad car, making inaudible sounds. The dim interior light of his cab betrayed him shaking his head, as he closed the door. Then, as slowly as he arrived, he drove off, leaving us standing silently alone in the glare of our lone headlights beneath the pulsing northern lights.

After he drove off, I could only wonder aloud to Barbi: "What kind of lawman would think he needed to guard a small uninhabited reach of Campbell Creek, in subzero temperatures, from a woman with a sack and a guy in a wheelchair, beneath the northern lights in January?" We both laughed long and hard while hand-cranking our ice cream mill past midnight.

Perhaps he too went home to his wife that night, wondering what kind of knuckleheads would be standing on the ice, in the freezing cold, defending a small bag of ice with an axe, so they could *eat* ice cream. As the bard Robert Service once wrote, "*...and the northern lights have seen queer sights...*"

CHAPTER EIGHT

A Portentous Omen for 1976

About January 24, 1976, I was at home absorbed with a picture I painted throughout the night, hoping to finish. Mt. Hood in Oregon loomed across the canvas in deep sunset, casting a reflection across Lost Lake. I had been consigned to paint it for an attorney in Portland, Oregon. The house was quiet. Barbi had been in town working the night shift at the hospital on Elmendorf AFB. Beyond the horizon of the painting, I was oblivious to the world around me. It was cold and overcast outside. An uncanny ambient light, which I'd failed to notice, filtered through the windows. I was content alone, wrapped up in my artwork. Had I noticed the time, I would have expected Barbi home at any moment.

Startling me, she burst through the door, followed by a rush of cold air. Noticeably alarmed, she asked "Have you looked outside lately?" Absorbed in a detail on the canvas, I didn't really hear what she said. However, the alarm in her voice didn't escape my notice.

I paused in the middle of a brush stroke. Then shifting my attention said, "What did you say?"

"Come and look out the window at this cloud!" she urged, an uneasy tone in her voice. "What do you think is happening?"

As far as I was concerned, nothing was happening other than I couldn't get the reflection of the mountain on the lake painted right. Her alarm didn't warrant anything less than a major earthquake. Obviously an earthquake hadn't occurred. Who on Earth ever gets that worked up over a cloud? She seemed to be overly dramatizing this cloud. Being torn between my painting and her demands made me cranky. Annoyed, I sauntered to the window, glancing toward where she pointed.

For a moment, I froze. The clouds from the southwest stretching to almost overhead were deep, dark purple, highlighted by a sinister reddish overtone. I ran outside, not even thinking to grab a jacket, with Barbi close behind me. The entire horizon was being swallowed by this phenomenon. Beneath it, the city of Anchorage was disappearing as if consumed by some final judgment. In all my years outdoors, I never saw anything even remotely approaching what gradually rolled over our heads. It was as if the hand of God had stirred red earth into blood, smearing it across the sky. Stunned, we stared in sober silence. What little sound there was in the woods seemed to fade into muffled oblivion.

To call it eerie understates the image overtaking us. It was astounding! I whispered to Barbi, "What is it?"

She gasped, "I don't know. I was driving down the highway, and it began to materialize from the southwest. Everybody on the highway saw it at the same time I did. It was creepy." She went on describing this weird manifestation. "As the traffic continued down the highway, everybody gradually slowed to a crawl as if reluctant to confront it! I slowed down to maybe 25 mph." Her final comment lapsed into somber silence. Then she asked me again, "What do you *think* it is?"

I knew a great deal about the natural world around me, but I was speechless even to guess. As we spoke, it continued to obfuscate the daylight around us.

"People driving down the highway all had to turn on their headlights to see," Barbi interjected with a sense of dread, as darkness began to engulf us. She hesitated, then continued stammering, "It's...like Judgment Day...proclaimed in the Bible."

Suddenly I noticed I was still holding a paintbrush in my hand. I wondered if Barbi was going to disappear in the Rapture, leaving me standing there alone. She was so quiet; I gave a furtive glance to my right to check if she was still behind me. "Did you try the radio to see if there were any news alerts?" I asked.

"Yes, I tried all the stations." she faintly replied, "There was nothing."

In those days, it wasn't hard to try all the stations in the span of a few seconds. It must be remembered that Alaska had just become a state seventeen years earlier. Anchorage was still on the edge of a frontier. Current news was always late. On the other hand, the Alaska *bush pipeline* was often more effective for transmitting news than all of our modern broadcasting. The *bush pipeline* was an amorphous word-of-mouth system that had been in effect since before history even knew about it. Sometimes it seemed to out-compete our most sophisticated news systems. An event might occur in Dutch Harbor in the Aleutian Islands, and folks in Nome could know about it in a matter of hours. A few days later, we'd hear about it on the evening news.

The next morning rose bright and sunny. Our entire world, though, was cast in a tan overtone. Examining this fine layer of tan snow, word came through the bush pipeline that Mt. St. Augustine, lying a couple of hundred miles to the southwest of Anchorage, had erupted and sent thousands of tons of ash ten thousand to fourteen thousand feet into the tropopause, drifting northeast over Anchorage and the surrounding areas.

On the evening news, we heard that from Iliamna to Anchorage, a quarter- to a half-inch of ash had been deposited over hundreds of square miles. Continuing through April, the mountain's eruption created havoc throughout the Cook Inlet Region. At one point, an ash blizzard completely stopped traffic in the Homer area. Although covered with succeeding snowfalls, the layers of ash could be seen in cross sections of snow the rest of the winter.

On Memorial Day weekend, we drove up to Mt. McKinley National Park. Our nice weekend weather went south, as we drove into the park as far as the Teklanika River. In those days, there wasn't the federal presence in the park during the off-season that there is today. The park was shut down for the winter, but the road was left open for travelers moving in and out of the town of Kashwitna on the other side of the park. Because winter lingered, we virtually had the place to ourselves.

The Teklanika still had about three feet of ice on it in places. The water, warmed with the approaching spring, cut deep channels into the river ice. Braided down the river were several leads where the ice had completely melted, exposing open water in the riverbed. The sky continued to be overcast, and it began to rain, with the temperatures in the high thirties and low forties. We set up a lean-to with a tarp and started looking for firewood to get supper cooking. Since it was still early spring for that country and wet everywhere, Barbi was worried that we wouldn't be able to find dry wood to build a fire. She looked out of sorts, as though we were facing a horrible weekend.

My thoughts flashed back to Troop 25 in Oregon years before, when I took the boys out on a camping trip in February. It had been raining for weeks. Everything was soggy wet. The boys and I hiked a short distance into a place on the Sandy River and set up camp. As we predicted, it started raining again. For a couple of hours, the boys struggled to build a campfire without success. Despairing, some of them launched into whining that the country was too wet. They wanted to go home. Their outburst reflected the feelings of the others, spiraling the whole troop downward. This soggy bunch of boys looked as reproachful as wet puppies.

I let them take the challenge as far as I knew they could, and then I interrupted their bellyaching. Raising my voice above their moaning, I challenged them, "I can build a fire on a mud puddle, using only one match and whatever I can find on the ground. If not, we'll go home." With water dripping off the brim of a few hats, this ostensibly rash statement was met with incredulous stares and silence. Water dripped from the vegetation, as I wondered how they would respond. This rallied them back into one unit as if the sun had burst upon them. In a lighter spirit, it became them against me, and they started looking for the largest puddle they could find. Some believed I'd do it; others wanting to go home didn't. Everything, including their clothing was damp, but this new challenge completely distracted them from the vexing weather.

In the meantime, I went over to an evergreen and cut enough green boughs to build a base up through a puddle. Then, chopping madly, I cut into an old wet log. At about four inches below the bark, I began to produce dry wood. Furiously, I cut out the dry wood, shoving it under my poncho as fast as I could to keep it dry. The boys were all eyes, amazed that there really was dry wood in the surrounding forest. Some even grabbed an axe and went off on their own to see if they could find dry wood by chopping deep into the center of a log.

Returning to camp, I whittled up a large pile of tinder and kindling from the dry wood tucked in the shelter of my poncho. The rain slowed to a drizzle. Laying sticks across the boughs, I built a platform above the water level.

Seeing this, the whiners detected their free trip home might not be a sure bet. They firmly reminded me that I could use only one match. By then, however, I'd won the majority to my side. They really wanted to see this fire roar up out of the water. Upon the platform I placed the huge pile of tinder and lit it while feeding in the kindling. Some of the boys were beginning to bring back dry wood they had chopped from logs. Others objected to their assistance. By then, though, it largely became a troop challenge we were waging against the force of nature. After about an hour of intense effort on my part, we had a roaring fire on a mud puddle.

As I looked up into the damp afternoon air, I caught a wisp of smoke coming up from a fire that some of the boys had begun building at their patrol site. My back was killing me, but the reward of seeing that smoke made it worthwhile. With three patrol fires and a main campfire burning, things began to look much better, despite the fact that the drizzle had gone back to rain.

Those boys learned two valuable lessons that weekend. First, tasks can often be accomplished in the face of despair and discouragement. Then as the sun broke out the next day, they learned that if they persevered, circumstances might change defeat to victory. They had a great weekend and didn't want to leave on Sunday.

In McKinley Park, I could see Barbi slipping into discouragement. I grabbed my axe and wandered from camp to an old uprooted tree stump and began to chop into it. The root ball was washed clean from many seasons of rain. I knew the stump was full of sap that would burn hot. Amazed, she watched as I gathered dry wood to build a fire. As I did, I couldn't help but think how easy it was going to be building a fire on the ground instead of in a puddle of water.

We donned our ponchos and cooked supper. The weekend was drizzly, and the temperatures dropped slightly. On Sunday night, I thought I could feel snow in the air. Keeping alert throughout the night, I occasionally woke, watching for the change I felt coming. Sure enough, about 5:30 that morning clouds dropped low over the river bottom in the distance rolling toward us. Abruptly shaking Barbi, I anxiously said, "Wake up! We've gotta get out of here. Snow's moving in on us."

Barbi looked around, objecting, "It doesn't look any different than it has all weekend. Can't we sleep another hour?"

"We drove into this area in my car, and I have no intentions of being stuck for a couple of extra days waiting for snow to melt," I told her. "We've gotta move fast."

By the time we had camp nearly taken down, the clouds were on us, with snow lacing through the wind. With a couple of drainage divides to cross, I suspected there'd be snow on the road. The last item to pack was the coffee pot. We poured one cup each for the trip out and used the coffee and dregs to douse the fire.

Out on the road, the snow began falling like a thick curtain with perhaps two inches of wet snow over the divides. The car, heavily loaded over the rear tires, spun only a few times, but we were pushing our luck. Back on the highway, we turned north and drove to the Healy Roadhouse for breakfast before heading home to Anchorage.

For months, we had seriously looked for a vehicle that we could trust in circumstances as we had just experienced, so on the way home we decided to buy a four-wheel drive vehicle. These sold for a premium in Alaska, running perhaps 25 percent over the prices in the lower 48 states. During one of my conversations with Dad in Portland, I asked him to keep an eye open for an International Scout. I'd carefully considered how I might load my chair into a Scout II and could do it with little difficulty.

Over the past eight years, I was growing accustomed to moving my wheelchair in the backcountry. While problematic, the challenges of getting out of difficult situations were becoming familiar. I knew I was ready to push my limits by traveling farther into the backcountry, using a four-wheel-drive vehicle.

Unlike me, Barbi seemed to have thoughts of the nurturing kind on her mind. We both loved having kids around the house. There seemed to be a constant flow of little people in and out of our house. Since Scott and I were close friends, it was natural that Sherry came to our trailer often. She loved to chitchat and sometimes provided me with a running monologue. I loved listening to her while painting a picture. She was fascinated with my artwork. She constantly brought pictures that she drew just for me. When Barbi came to Alaska and met Sherry, they took to each other.

During the interim, Pat, a single mom with a seven-year-old daughter named Renée, moved west of Scott's trailer. Renée was a pretty girl with dark hair, and although she and Sherry were close in age, Renée was taller. She was charming and warmed up to me as a father image. Renée and Sherry became inseparable, and so it was naturally no accident for Renée to be at our house a great amount of time talking about whatever was going on in her life. Together, they flirted and carried on, and I dished it back teasing them unmercifully. When they thought they were getting the upper hand, I'd feign a move toward them, sending them shrieking for cover or squealing out of the house. Soon, they'd be back for more.

When I first met Scott, I nicknamed Sherry "Kitten." Now that Renee and Sherry were such close friends, Renée wanted a nickname. Laughing, I said, "Okay, Tadpole." She brightened, finally feeling part of our inner circle. We loved Sherry and Renée like our own kids. It was a good time in our lives. As time went on, our house attracted other kids like a magnet. We both enjoyed the pitter-patter of their little feet running the hall, chattering and laughing.

Earlier, we had filed for adoption through the state of Alaska, but the waiting period was five years. During the winter, we talked about trying our hand as foster parents. Considering that we both loved children, we felt we had lots of love to give foster children. In view of this goal, Barbi quit her job at Elmendorf, and we filed the necessary paperwork to become foster parents. The last step was a home visit by a state social worker. By the time we came to the home visit, I was beginning to think there was no end to what those people wanted to know.

Barbi made sure the house was crystal clean for the day of the visit. The dogs were tied up outside, so they wouldn't muddy our visitor and perhaps give us a demerit. We cleared the yard of sticks and bones the dogs had drug in, and tidied everything up outside. We were on pins and needles, especially Barbi.

Then the moment arrived. A car pulled into the driveway, and a smartly dressed social worker emerged. Looking very professional with a small satchel, she headed for the front door. I thought Barbi and I looked like Ward and June Cleaver on the television comedy, *Leave it to Beaver.* Actually, in my estimation, the whole affair was a bit pretentious. Out of pure nervousness, I hid my discomfort by acting lighthearted toward the situation. It was all I could do just to keep from touching off some humor that would insert a bit of levity, as the lady walked into the living room.

The questions droned on, making me feel like this very stoic gal was hunting in July for a piece of ice thrown out in January. She went on with an air of superiority and not a hint of enthusiasm in all this absurdity. Barbi, sitting poised and proper, slightly nestled into me, played the role of a perfect first-time mother. A little more casually situated, I had my arm relaxed around her, resting it on the back of the couch where we were sitting.

Finally, in a sincerely patronizing tone, this gal said with some closure, "Now, we know that all married couples have disagreements from time to time, and so I can safely assume you two do also. Therefore, how do you handle these disagreements?"

I wondered who the '*we*' might be. I decided this gal has to smile at least once before she leaves.

As Barbi opened her mouth to respond in a nice polite manner, a spark of humor ignited my thoughts like a match to propane. Shifting my arm, I strained to reach behind the couch, while saying in a matter-of-fact tone, "Well, you see, I have this belt with hooks in it back here and..."

Barbi immediately interrupted me with, "David!!! What are you saying?"

Horrified, that poor social worker rose an inch off her seat and froze, her mouth aghast in pure dread. A funnier sight I had never seen on the face of another woman in all my life. I started laughing. If it had been any other circumstance, Barbi would have belted me a good one.

The social worker immediately *hoped* I was joking. She twitched a slight nervous smile, as Barbi tried to recover the situation. Looking at me, Barbi blurted out, "Tell her the truth!"

I began back-peddling, thinking, *oh boy, you've done it now!* I assured the poor lady that there wasn't really a belt behind the couch, while suppressing my laughter. Nervously, she tried to laugh, but I could see she was struggling between jumping up and gawking behind the couch or bolting for the front door. At that, I invited her to come and see for herself, but the humor was actually beginning to infect her, and she settled back on her chair. As for her question, I guess she got a live answer.

The conversation lightened up, continuing afterward on a much brighter note. There were even a few more smiles and chuckles, as we wrapped up the interview. We served some coffee and generally visited without the intensity we felt at the beginning of her visit.

After she left, I sure got an earful. Barbi was struck with the idea that we had just been written off the prospective foster parent list. Being a pretty good judge of people, however, I was certain she was wrong. Amazingly, we were immediately approved after our home study with the social worker.

Our application and approval was for children zero to two years old. The first placement they needed help with, however, was Davy, an amiable little nine-year-old boy with a moderately severe case of cerebral palsy. He had never been in a foster home for more than six months, and they needed to place him again. His limitations had caused doctors to believe he was blind until he was five. The state also believed he was mentally retarded. They pleaded with us to take him into our care, thinking that my impairment might help us to understand him and perhaps give him some encouragement.

Our deliberation over his age and impairment raised some concerns. I wasn't sure I could even remotely respond to his needs. But, talking it over, we finally agreed to open our home to this little guy.

He was supposed to arrive on the following Monday, but an urgent need arose, and the social worker called on Friday afternoon, asking if we could take him that evening. We'd made arrangements to go out to dinner with several couples, so Barbi called me at work, presenting the dilemma. After discussing it briefly, we agreed to accept Davy right away.

From his first arrival in our home, he was a delight, and we immediately made him part of our lives. He went out with us that evening and stole the hearts of everyone at the restaurant.

He quickly fell into a routine in our home. The school bus began picking him up at our trailer house on Monday morning. Whenever we went somewhere, he went with us. For me, it was difficult at first. I felt way over my head. Still adjusting to my own condition, I was confronted with another's serious physical problem. As I focused on Davy, though, my own problems seemed to dwarf.

We soon developed a hunch that Davy was smarter than we had been led to believe. This intrigued us, and we looked for ways to draw out his intelligence by requiring more out of him. Rather than resist us or return a dull stare, he gave us a wide smile and exceeded our expectations. We quickly realized that he had only been rising to the level of what others had expected of him. He'd act irrational only as a defense mechanism.

We also took him into the outdoors with us. Though the cerebral palsy caused him difficulty, he mustered everything he could give to overcome barriers. One of his difficulties was walking. He tended to walk on the ball of his feet. As a result, every task he took on was a new challenge, and he constantly amazed us with what he could accomplish. We cut him even less slack, and he always measured up to our expectations. Afterward, his wide smile told us, 'thank you for believing in me.' It wasn't long before he started affectionately calling us Momma and Daddy.

Fur Rendezvous in Anchorage in the 1970s was a spectacular occasion. The event drew tourists from all across the United States. It also drew trappers and traders from deep within Alaska's bush. To them, it was a time of seeing old friends, carousing, engaging in untamed frivolity, and selling a year's supply of accumulated goods to tourists and fur buyers. Bush folks, sometimes in rough rural attire, brushed shoulders with urbanites wearing flimsy clothing and carrying cameras. In such a distinct mix of metropolitan and rural culture, people didn't always understand each other or try to get along. The mix of people and events created a turbulence of activity.

Barbi, Davy, and I decided to go into Anchorage for this event. Davy was enchanted by the colors and imagery surrounding him and the bustle of activity. To him, everyone was a friend, and he charmed anyone he could. He quickly ran out of steam, however, due to the energy he put into walking. Thus, we began to slow our progress through the crowds. When he became tired, I told him to jump onto my lap. Davy and I then shot off through the crowd with Barbi in tow. It was as if someone was giving him a ride in a hot air balloon. It stirred him to high spirits and laughter.

Racing down the sidewalk with Davy sitting on my lap and cheering us along, we captured instant attention from the crowd. There were still no curb ramps in Anchorage. By then, however, jumping up and down curbs was second nature to me. So when we came to a curb, I would pop a wheelie and proceed along, oblivious to onlookers.

Barbi was amused by the looks of horror on people's faces. Folks would jump to catch me from going over backward, but I was traveling so fast, they would come up with air. Others would grab their hearts. The first time I jumped off a curb, Davy was slightly unraveled. Afterward, though, it delighted him, and he wanted to jump every curb in Anchorage. Occasionally as I popped a wheelie, Davy could see someone nearby gasp or jump out of the way. This brought waves of laughter from him.

Whenever we stopped at a trader's stand, Davy would climb down to examine all the wonderful pieces of art the bush folks brought in to sell. And so, Davy was up and down from my lap the rest of the day. Pretty soon Barbi started getting tired. "Can I sit on your lap too?"

"Momma, you can't sit here. I'm here!" he laughed, which brought a chuckle from both of us. By the time we arrived home, we were a pretty tired family.

On Mother's Day, Barbi wanted to take a ride up the Turnagain Arm for a picnic in the woods. The Turnagain Arm is a saltwater fiord that runs into the mountains past Anchorage to the east. Foul weather from the ocean tended to pack in at the head of the fiord.

When we arrived, it started raining. Davy was in high spirits, but Barbi became gloomy and saw it as thwarting the occasion. I tried to treat the rain lightheartedly, and we found a semi-dry place under trees.

We built a fire and threw up a small lean-to with a large space blanket from my survival gear. Davy, impervious to the rain, kept looking from me to Barbi, sensing something wasn't as it should be. Laying some blankets on the ground under the lean-to, we huddled under the space blanket and warmed by the fire. We ate our picnic, listening to the rain sizzle in the fire.

On one of her visits to us, Lois introduced Davy to Cat Steven's music, and he loved it. His favorite song was "Peace Train." He loved to dance to its tune. Barbi used this to encourage him to do as much as he could to get himself ready for school in the mornings. If ready before the bus arrived, they enjoyed a special time together. Loading the LP, *The Very Best of Cat Stevens,* into the record player, she played "Peace Train." The two of them laughed, cavorting around the living room, holding hands. Breathless and confident, he would mount the steps of the school bus and wave back at Barbi, ready for a new day.

Over time, we could see that much of Davy's physical struggle could be mitigated if his Achilles tendons were stretched. We were told that when he was younger, he underwent a successful procedure to stretch the tendons out longer. As he grew, though, they caused him an increasing amount of trouble.

Barbi took him to a doctor to check into having this remedied. At the hospital, Davy slipped into his defensive reaction, hiding his intelligence. After seeing Davy, the doctor who worked for the state of Alaska would not recommend the procedure. He said he didn't want to waste the state's money. It was a price people often paid for socialized medicine. Barbi was furious with the doctor and the system, with the result that we were labeled overprotective foster parents. All things being equal, we set about investigating how we might help Davy with or without the state's assistance.

Several weeks after I called Dad about a vehicle, he returned my call telling me he'd found a 1973 Scout II that was just what we were looking for. We sent him the money and some Alaskan license plates, and the vehicle was ours. Now we had to get the Scout to Alaska. All options required vigorous return travel over two thousand five hundred miles one way. We knew we were facing long days of driving and nights out in the wilderness where we'd put up a quick camp. Davy was having more difficulty moving about, and the state didn't seem to hold out any hope toward helping him.

He would give the trip his best, but we knew that it would take a hard toll on him physically. We discussed this with the social worker to see how the state might help us resolve the conundrum. They seemed eager to come to our aid and decided to assign him temporary quarters until we returned. Then he could come under our care once again.

Barbi really wanted to bring Davy along, but I was reluctant. The intensity of my struggles still left me unsure of my ability. I didn't want to compromise him. The state seemed to be offering a reasonable solution, so we arranged to leave Davy in Anchorage.

In May, we left for the lower 48 to collect the Scout in combination with a vacation. My brother Jerry was also graduating from high school that spring. We said goodbye to Davy, letting him know we'd be back in a month.

Barbi and I then flew south. On our arrival, Mom asked where Davy was. We had written so much about him and shared about his progress over the phone that they were anxious to see him. To say the least, they were very disappointed he was not with us. With belated second thoughts, I felt bad at the airport about not bringing him. Intuitively, it just didn't feel right for him not to be with us. He'd become part of our family. We hoped that he was being well cared for.

The next day I installed hand controls in the Scout. The job went quickly. I had gathered a lot of experience at it by this time. Once installed, we were independent and at our leisure. The Scout handled well, providing the freedom we looked for in a four-wheel drive.

After Jerry's graduation ceremony, we convened at a pizza parlor in Portland to celebrate. We made up a large group, filling the ranks on several tables pushed together. Barbi had been horseback riding all that day with Jerry and walked a little bow-legged. Coming back from the washroom, she passed a team of minor league baseball players in another section of the restaurant. These guys were into their cups celebrating. One of them made a derisive remark about how she was walking. Busy visiting with someone next to me, the event entirely escaped my notice. However, Dad was in a line of sight of Barbi's return. While he didn't hear what was said, he immediately saw that it embarrassed her.

Dad quietly rose and intercepted her. He asked what had happened. Armed with the insult she received, he headed off alone toward these nine baseball players. By then, Barbi had returned to the table, visibly embarrassed, and told us what just happened. I still didn't notice Dad was missing. Then I heard him across the restaurant retort with a steely calm imperative, "Fellow, I think you'd better apologize to the young lady!" Chairs were suddenly being pushed back, as men rose to make a stand with the guy Dad directed his comment toward. They were obviously trying to intimidate Dad by their numbers.

Looking up in time to see Jerry shoot off toward Dad, I pushed away from the table. Barbi asked, "Where are you going?"

"I'll be back in a minute," I quietly replied, not wanting to draw any attention to myself. Obviously a fight was materializing. Jerry quickly worked his way around to Dad's left with my brother Keith completing the flanking maneuver to his right. Working my chair around to the opposite side of the restaurant, I came up behind the team. Searching for an equalizer, I grabbed a wooden chair in one hand and held it off to one side, intending to hurl it if things went sour.

We were grossly outnumbered, and the moment was tense. Nobody spoke a word. Glancing around, the troublemaker slowly awakened to the fact that perhaps he was just a bit out of line.

Again Dad said in a calmer tone, "I think you owe the lady an apology."

I saw it slowly dawn on the culprit that a fight was going to be the ugly outcome of his remark. As abruptly as the incident started, he backed down.

With an air of insouciance, the fellow walked over to Barbi, who was chagrined at being the potential source of a donnybrook in the restaurant, and politely apologized. The situation was diffused. Shortly thereafter, they all paid their bill, bellowing about how unfriendly the place was, and walked out of the restaurant.

Dad, Jerry, Keith, and I resumed the celebration, not giving it another thought. The ladies on the other hand, discussed the incident for some time afterward.

Keith turned fifteen that spring, and we invited him to help us drive the Scout back to Alaska. Driving to Seattle, we loaded the Scout below deck on the Alaska flagship M/V *Columbia*, embarking from Washington to Haines, Alaska. Traveling in the steerage class, we laid our bedrolls on the deck in a common area. Sleep, while people were milling around all night, was impossible.

The second day, we searched until we found a quiet place on the open mid-ship deck. It was a narrow, isolated place adjacent to the gunwale on the starboard side. Spreading our bedrolls on the deck, we watched the frigid sea waves roll directly below us. In all, we spent four nights onboard ship. As the ship pitched and swayed across the miles of sea waves, I consoled myself with the wisdom of leaving Davy in Anchorage. At night, the ship's engines vibrated beneath us in a steady drone, and the sea spray moistened the air while we slept on the deck. If Davy had come along, it would have been dangerous for him.

With no money to spare, we traveled on a shoestring budget. Midway through the voyage, we were forced to ration our funds even more conservatively, or we wouldn't have enough to buy fuel on the way home. When the ship docked at various ports, we resorted to buying hotdogs and bologna with some bread and a little cheese to get to the next town.

Arriving in Haines late, we headed into the wilderness, searching for a place to spend the night. A couple of hours later, we pulled into a quiet little place that looked like a picture of serenity. The mosquitoes were out in hordes. Lingering in the Scout for a moment with the windows closed tight, we knew our fate as mosquito fodder. I remembered seeing a bear run across our path right before we landed for the night. I'm sure he was running from mosquitoes. Flinging the doors open, we hit the ground running for a location to build a smoky fire quickly. Smoke eliminated about 90 percent of them. However, the remaining 10 percent of a hundred thousand is still an abysmal threat. Once the fire was built, we set up our camp in marginal sanity.

There wasn't much interest expressed for the hotdogs we had for supper that night. Keith's eyes just kind of glossed over, as he thought of eating another hotdog. It was good to sleep on ground that didn't vibrate beneath us, but it seemed that we had traded the drone of the ship's engines for the low hum of mosquitoes. They incessantly hummed their bloodthirsty tune throughout the night. It was as if in one single low and subtle scream of starvation, cannibals searched the woods in frenzied hordes for fresh meat.

The road through Canada in those early years was not paved. Furthermore, the Canadians didn't appear to give it much attention until the spring moisture drained out of the roadbed in late June or July. We discovered that the spring moisture was still abundant in the roadbed, as we headed for Alaska. Consequently, we were in four-wheel drive and compound low gear for hundreds of miles. The fastest we traveled was 25 mph, and that was only for short stretches. Along much of the road we worked hard to avoid ruts created by semi-trucks. Ruts that those trucks dug into the roadbed looked like canyons next to the Scout. Any one of them could have high-centered the Scout. It was awful! Driving twelve hours each day, it took several days. When we crossed the border into Alaska and drove onto the paved road surface, I felt like we were floating on air. I never realized I had such a secret affinity for paved roads until then.

We were now on the last stretch home, free of the harshest part of our travels. We would soon see Davy. Arriving home, we gave the Alaska Social Services a call. What we discovered utterly devastated us. While we were stateside, the Social Service folks decided to place Davy under permanent custody in an institution. They believed it was too hard on him to keep moving from home to home. We were not allowed to see him or know where he was. Naively we had assumed he could rejoin us when we arrived back in Anchorage. We suffered terrible guilt for leaving him and felt helpless to resolve the situation. We were young and didn't have enough sense to press an objection with the state.

We never saw Davy again. Losing Davy to the state's system is still the biggest regret of my life and will disturb me to the end of my days. Like the Mt. St. Augustine's ash that hung over Anchorage earlier in the year, this loss has hung over us throughout our lives. The pain of his loss still bears heavy after more than thirty years. I can't listen to "Peace Train" without a wellspring of good memories and tears. I often wonder what became of him; how he's doing; if he's happy; and wish things had worked out differently. We hadn't lived enough years then to know what we know now, or events would certainly not have turned out the way they did.

With many years of struggle in a wheelchair now behind me, I believe I would have given more weight to the adventure he would have experienced on the trip, over that of protecting him from the physical harm it would have caused him. The only solace we have today is praying for Davy. We can only trust that a loving God, who has governed our affairs throughout these years, also loves and has been concerned for Davy over the same period of time.

CHAPTER NINE

Humbled by Mud

Earlier in the spring before Davy joined us, I had helped a friend, Bill Smith, replace the engine in his Jeep. As the summer headed into fall, I discovered that my car, a 1967 Dodge Dart, needed its 220 slant-six engine replaced. After Keith left, I rented a hoist and pulled the engine. Without the luxury of a garage, I spread a tarp over the gravel driveway and worked alone. Once out, I loaded the old engine into the Scout and exchanged it for a rebuilt engine.

When lowering the rebuilt back in the Dodge, I couldn't get myself positioned up into the engine compartment enough to rock it into place. It was yet another matter bringing to focus my limitations. Each time I had to face insurmountable limitations, those feelings of incompetency once again surfaced, leaving me empty inside. Suppressing those feelings really didn't help, but I could find no profit in dwelling on them. They stayed hidden within me unresolved and abetted a growing anger. Cursing and swearing at the engine, I finally conceded to doing something repulsive to me. Ask for help.

When September rolled around the BLM sent me to Phoenix, Arizona, for four weeks of training in the field of administrative law. Barbi drove me to the airport in Anchorage. She planned to fly down in a few weeks and spend the rest of the time with me, and we would fly back home together.

I knew the days would be hot in Phoenix, but I still wasn't prepared for it. I registered at the Granada Royal Hotel and discovered that the room had a full kitchen. Wanting to avoid going back into the heat, I cooked supper in my room. I decided to rest until 10:00 p.m. and then take a long walk in the cool night air. Later when I walked outside, the cool night air was 105 °. Never having experienced anything like that, I found it disorienting. My walk was not as pleasant as I hoped it would be. Thereafter, I drove to some higher elevation in the evenings to escape the city heat.

The following weekend, I left the Phoenix area altogether, exploring the mountain country to the north. My favorite sanctuary became the Oak Creek area and the Cathedral Rocks. In those years, it was not populated as it is today. I found some lonely place and stopped for the night. The next morning, rising early and enjoying the cooler mountain air, I boiled coffee and cooked breakfast. This became my weekend routine. Afterward, there was always another mountain and distant horizon beckoning me. Exploring the desert, I really began to believe I could do the fieldwork of a realty specialist for the BLM.

Four weeks after I arrived in Arizona, I picked Barbi up at the Phoenix airport. She was as overwhelmed by the heat as I was, although I had adjusted to it a little bit. The heat was so intense; we needed to be extremely careful to avoid being burned by the car seats. From that experience, neither of us ever wanted to live anywhere near Phoenix or, for that matter, in the Southwestern United States. We were happy to return to Anchorage away from the heat of Arizona.

Midway through the winter, I was sent to Fairbanks to work in the BLM's records branch. I took the Scout and drove the Parks Highway. It was a trying journey in deep winter conditions, taking me twelve hours. Many of the roadhouses were closed. The temperatures were extremely cold in Fairbanks, and the sun didn't come up more than a finger above the horizon at high noon. I settled into a hotel room in town that night while the temperatures lingered deep into the subzero range.

While Barbi kept the home fires burning in Anchorage, I traveled more frequently for the BLM. The prospect of the BLM sending me to Arizona for more schooling in administrative law increased. Whenever I flew to the lower 48, I would pull the hand controls from the Scout, pack them in a bag, fly to my destination, and install them into a rental car. (Rental car companies didn't equip cars with hand controls during those years like many do today.) It would take ten or fifteen minutes to remove the hand controls and an hour to an hour and a half to install them in a rental car. While this wasn't difficult, I searched for easier ways to travel.

Whenever possible, I combined a work trip to Arizona with a vacation back to Oregon, and Barbi would join me. As stateside trips increased in frequency, Barbi and I thought it was a good idea to buy a vehicle to keep in the lower 48 some place. We mentioned this to Phil, a close friend I knew who once worked in Alaska. We kept in contact with him after he moved to the outskirts of Seattle. He offered to keep a vehicle for us in his orchard if we needed a place to park it.

During the spring of 1977, on vacation, we wanted to look for real estate in Eastern Oregon or Idaho where we might invest toward retirement someday. I also wanted to look over some of the areas the BLM administered and get a feel for whether I could do field work in those areas. In view of these goals, we flew to Portland in May and began looking for a vehicle we could use in our quest. A short time later, we found a 1970 Dodge pickup that once belonged to the U.S. Forest Service, Zigzag Ranger District. The pickup had a long, narrow box with a step side indentation on both sides of the bed behind the cab. It was a basic pickup with the bare essential rubber floor mats, no radio or air conditioner. On the other hand, it had low mileage, was a fine-looking truck in good running condition. Furthermore the price was right.

I had wanted a pickup since high school, but was discouraged on the idea for lack of a place to put a wheelchair. I schemed up many ideas to make it work for me. Some paraplegics would climb in on the passenger side of the pickup, haul their chair into the cab and slide across the seat. This seemed cumbersome and having the chair in the cab didn't appeal to me. Besides, now that I was married it would really be unmanageable with Barbi in the cab. Furthermore, I didn't want to inconvenience her with having to load my chair in and out of the back of the truck. Loading a chair from behind the seat on the driver's side was advantageous but awkward. It was unrealistic with a pickup. Granted, it was easier with the Scout than some other vehicles we owned, but I decided a wheelchair rack behind the cab of a step side pickup was a workable solution. By building a swing-out rack, I believed it possible to load and store my chair on the outside of the truck.

As I previously mentioned, Dad, a machinist, taught me to use the tools of his trade. As a result, I was no stranger to the tools needed to create this rack from scratch. Working in the driveway at my folks' house for a couple of days, I laid out the materials and went to work. Using an acetylene torch to weld the steel angle iron together, I began to make it take form. Dad's suggestion to inlay it with plywood backing gave it structural support.

It worked exactly as I envisioned it. Sitting in the driver's seat, I swung the rack out 90° to the cab. Then, lifting the folded chair, I hung it on the rack and swung it back nearly flush with the cab and rear fender, securing it with a bungee cord. To me, that simple adaptation was a major accomplishment. For the first time in nine years, I didn't need to pull a chair into a vehicle with me. After installing a permanent set of hand controls in the pickup, we were set to roll.

My brother Jerry worked on the McKay ranch outside of Jordan Valley, Oregon. Don and Bess McKay had a summer ranch in the high country. When we arrived, Bess mentioned she wanted to get up there and square it away for the summer season. Jerry and Don were working cattle, so Barbi and I volunteered to drive Bess to the upper place and help her. The spring grass was chasing the snowdrifts from the high country, leaving the ground wet. Although it had been frosty in the morning, a deep blue sky and bright sun promised a warm day. It was perhaps 10:00 a.m. when we finally left the main ranch house.

Gaining elevation, the road changed from graded gravel to dirt and finally into a two-track. Not far from the summer ranch, we came upon a low meadow that looked like a good place to get stuck. Stopping on high ground, we surveyed it and saw fresh tracks straight across it. They didn't even make an impression in the ground. It seemed as though the meadow was wetter than that, but rather than get out and walk across it as I should have, I gave the truck a little boost and drove onto it at a good clip. As soon as my tires hit the edge of the meadow, I could feel them being sucked into the mud-like pudding. My response was to give it more gas. Someone else had recently been across here, I reasoned, so it couldn't be that bad.

Naturally, this was the wrong thing to do. It really was bad. We bogged down to a halt about fifty feet from the dry ground at the edge of the meadow. I knew we were seriously stuck. Unloading my wheelchair from the side of the pickup, I jumped from the truck to run around to the back. The mud grabbed my wheels, oozing around my spokes, as I watched the whole pickup slowly sink to the floorboards and the bumpers. A sick feeling grew in the pit of my stomach. Pulling the handyman jack from the back of the truck, we dug into the mud enough to get the jack under the bumper.

For those unacquainted with a handyman jack, a brief description is in order. These jacks are as vital to survival in rural America as an axe. They work on a ratchet principle, weigh twenty to thirty pounds, and are about thirty-six inches long. Most are rated to hoist several tons. A long pipe handle about twenty-four inches long works the jack. I need to say here that handyman jacks are extremely dangerous. Letting them get out of hand has seriously injured many men. I do not recommend it as a tool for someone unfamiliar with it.

In the bog, I ratcheted the jack handle to raise the bumper, but the foot of the jack drove into the ground as easily as pushing a forty-penny nail into a can of axle grease. This was not going to be a good day. It took some work to pull the jack out of the mud. Next we dug a wide hole in the mud. Dragging the spare tire from the bed of the truck, we set it on its side in the hole as a base for the jack.

All this time, I was becoming far more intimate with the cold mud than I wanted to be. I felt like the fox with Brer Rabbit's tar baby. It was caking on the wheels of my chair and balling up in the palm of my gloves making it difficult to grab the wheels and maneuver around the jack. Those leather gloves felt like they weighed two pounds each. Every foot or two, I needed to rub my glove palms across the spokes of my chair to scrape the mud off enough to get a grip on the wheels and move the chair. Frustrated with my inability to move about freely, I became exasperated even more for not having walked over the ground before trying to drive across it.

When I tried again to jack the rear bumper of the truck up, to my amazement the spare tire started sinking into the mud because the mud had a firm airlock on the vehicle's tires. At that point, Bess offered to walk over the ridge to a ranch a mile and a half away. If no one was there, there was another ranch that far again farther down country. Barbi said she'd accompany Bess, and they both left me there alone to do what I could. I hated asking for help, but delaying seemed unprofitable. As I surveyed the mess I got us into, the two of them soon disappeared out of sight. In the meantime, I tried to reset the tire farther under the truck to use it again as a base for the jack.

Time ticked away. My back was screaming at me, as I looked at my watch. They were gone for quite awhile, leaving me to reckon they must have walked to the next ranch. By and by, I found I was getting nowhere. I simply couldn't break the airlocks holding the tires. Loading the jack and tire back in the pickup, I sat waiting for their return. By then, my chair was laden with mud, and it seemed the more the day wore on, the thicker the mud became.

With little to do but wait, I studied my predicament. The truck was in a real mess. I was a mess, covered from head to wheel. Moreover, Barbi and Bess had to walk out for help because of me. Doubt piled its ugly weight, condemning me as I sat there alone. In all my previous years of outdoor living, I gained much inner strength from the land, but it all failed me in times like this. Nature wasn't providing the inner strength I searched for. Feeling incompetent, the emptiness inside manifested itself. Confinement to a chair seemed to magnify my shortcomings. If I had my legs under me, I was sure I could do something more. Helpless, even waiting could pull me into despair and anger. Shaking those thoughts from my head, I again buried them. On the surface, people saw a calloused veneer. Beneath it, though, lay incurable hopelessness I lived with daily knowing I'd never walk again.

I wiped those remnant thoughts from my mind when I heard a vehicle coming over the ridge. Soon, a four-wheel drive crested the ridge with Bess, Barbi, and Ben, a rancher who dropped what he was doing to come help us out of the mud. Walking toward the edge of the meadow, I intercepted them. He seemed to be a real nice guy, as we discussed what to do. We sure appreciated his help.

There were two chains in my truck, and he had one. He thought if he didn't get too close, he'd be able to hook those chains together and pull us free. Backing into the meadow as close as he dared, he pulled a chain from his vehicle. Dragging out the two logging chains from our truck, we hooked them all together and stepped into our respective vehicles. As he pulled the chains taut, I accelerated the truck, hopelessly spinning the wheels. It was no use, the airlock on my tires held a firm grip, as he buried his four-wheel-drive vehicle up to the hubs.

Thinking to myself, *I'm not the only one that was going to have a bad day,* I killed the engine. Anger burned within me. Ben took it in stride though, not saying much. Actually, it was one of those moments when it's a real fine idea not to say much. He shook his head and said he'd walk back to the ranch and return with a tractor.

An hour later, he returned with a huge tractor that had rear wheels that were higher than my head. This time, we kept the tractor on high ground and stretched a cable to his vehicle. Latched to the front of his four-wheel drive vehicle, the tractor began to pull.

It put an enormous strain on the 4x4. Abruptly the air-locked wheels released their grip, and his vehicle, driven by Bess, popped out of the mud while the tractor shot off up the hill. The same thing occurred with our pickup. It seemed for a moment that the tractor would split my truck in two. Then with a throat-sucking sound, the airlock released. I suddenly found myself steering backward at a speed I would not have chosen for this particular evacuation. Consequently, I whipped all over the meadow spraying mud everywhere. On dry ground, I slammed on my brakes, nearly hitting the four-wheel drive parked to the side.

By the time we were free from the mud, it was late afternoon. We humbly conveyed our appreciation to Ben for his help, apologizing for the trouble we caused him. He didn't mind, however, graciously taking it in stride, not showing the least bit of animosity toward my stupidity. That made it even worse. A good cussing would have made me feel better. He seemed to be a man of honor, not given to that sort of thing.

Turning the truck around to head back, I stared at those fresh tracks made earlier by an unknown driver. I wondered how it was possible that someone had crossed there without sinking in that mud. Back at the McKay ranch, Bess scrambled to get supper going while I used a garden hose to clean the mud from my wheelchair. By then, most of it had caked on hard. When Jerry arrived he looked at my truck, then at me. He wisely didn't ask, and I was in no mood to talk about what had happened. He shrugged, walked into the house, and cleaned up for supper.

Even with Barbi's help, we ate a very late supper. As the story emerged from Barbi and Bess around the table that evening, I was both chagrined and irked at myself for having to be pulled out of a bad spot. Jerry and Don were all ears, smiling and nodding, each no doubt reflecting on their own experiences getting stuck in the past. I couldn't say much. Stupid hurts. I winced at the gentle ribbing I received. It would become only one of a few times that I needed to be pulled from a tight spot.

In bed that night, I lay awake speculating how a vehicle went across that meadow without as much as making a half inch rut. The next morning, the thermometer revealed the answer. The temperatures still dropped pretty cold at night, freezing the surface of the ground hard. Someone must have driven across the meadow early that morning, before the sun had thawed the ground. I tucked that valuable information away for another time.

In the meantime, the weekend was coming up, and Jerry had Saturday afternoon off. Jordan Valley rolled its sidewalks up in the evenings, not offering much for nighttime entertainment. So the three of us decided to go into Caldwell, Idaho, and see what action we could find. (Caldwell was still more of a ranch and farm community in those years. The interstate highway had not been built yet, and the main flow of traffic still traveled along old U.S. 30.) The three of us loaded into our pickup, heading for the big town down in the valley. Rolling down the highway, we listened to Chris LeDoux tapes from a portable cassette player on the dashboard. Craning around the cab from the bed of the truck, Bear let her ears flap in the wind, as we sped along.

In Caldwell, we first hit a western clothing store and then fueled the truck for the return trip. After that, we went to a Chinese restaurant and then stopped at a dance hall. After a few drinks, Barbi and I joined some other folks on the dance floor. Although I couldn't use my legs, I was fairly good at spinning my chair about with Barbi on my arm. Not surprisingly, this brought us a great deal of attention. Folks weren't accustomed to seeing a guy in a wheelchair moving about on a dance floor. After the initial shock, though, they encouraged us on into the night. In fact, my dancing from a wheelchair was such a novelty that other women wanted to dance with me also. So when Barbi became tired, and we returned to our table, the gals drifted over one by one, asking me to dance with them. Not wanting to hurt any feelings, I obliged and kept the dance floor warm. After a few rounds with these friendly Idaho gals, my bride wasn't the least bit happy. When she objected, I became a bit claustrophobic in the smoke-filled dancehall and needed to get some fresh air.

Although we were having a great time, I still wasn't at ease being around people pressed in tight quarters. I excused myself, leaving Barbi with Jerry, and wandered outside to breathe the cool night air.

Before we went into the dancehall, we had draped a tarp over our gear, leaving Bear under it. The tarp was just hanging loose over the two sides and tailgate as a polite way of alerting folks not to be overly concerned with what was in the truck. I knew Bear would guard it for us. Walking over to the truck, I looked around to make sure everything was okay.

Bear somehow knew I was approaching. She went over to where I approached to lie in wait. When I lifted the corner of the tarp, she lunged up, poking her head out, happy to see me. Scratching behind her ears, I was alone with Bear, with the commotion from the dancehall muted behind us. After a few minutes, I returned to the dance hall. By then, the friendly Idaho ladies were occupying themselves elsewhere.

About 11:00 p.m., I needed to get another breath of good clean Idaho air. Moving into the shadows where I could scan the parking lot, I let my eyes adjust to the darkness. Soon I saw movement in the shadows perhaps fifty feet away. Melting back into a dark corner, I watched as a guy started moving toward the bed of our truck. Apparently he hadn't noticed me come outside.

The moon cast a blue tone across the parking lot. This guy leaned against my truck and lit a match, and I saw a puff of smoke go up behind his cupped hand. A streetlight cast a yellow glow down on the dancehall sign and the entrance to the parking lot. Everywhere else was dark. A vehicle turned in, momentarily sweeping its headlights across the parking lot, pulled up, and stopped. The guy with the cigarette stood back, temporarily fading from our truck like a ghost into the darkness. On guard in the shadows, I watched as the couple from the car disappeared into the dancehall. They had walked right by without seeing me.

The guy reemerged from the shadows, once again leaning on the side of my truck. It was obvious by now he wasn't intent on minding his own business, so I waited to see what he'd do. Actually, I should say I waited to see what Bear would do. I laughed silently to myself, as my mind played out the details that would follow if he didn't keep to himself. After a few more draws on the cigarette, he quietly lifted the tarp, exhaling smoke from the corner of his mouth. As I suspected, Bear was waiting for him, primed and ready to launch. Bear was black as coal so the man didn't see her coming, and she made no sound. She shot up, latching onto his nose, holding him tight in her teeth.

I had seen her grab another guy by the nose once when he was trying to become too familiar with the Scout. Then as now, I could see Bear making intense eye contact, capturing his undivided attention as only a Border Collie can do.

Instantly, I stepped out of the shadows, projecting a deep steady voice, "Sometimes it's healthier to keep your nose where it belongs." At the sound of my voice, Bear released her hold. The man grabbed his nose and made tracks for a place I suspected he felt a little safer. Bear then came into full view with her front feet up on the side of the pickup. I could hear her tail furiously sweeping against the underside of the tarp as I approached. I have heard coyotes laugh in the wild, and I've seen Border Collies smile. Bear was doing both that night as if to say, 'Eh, boss, we showed him, didn't we?!'

CHAPTER TEN

Sheik of the North

Late that summer, Dad called, saying he had some extra vacation time. Near the first of July, he packed up his bags and caught a flight to Anchorage. Barbi and I picked him up at the airport, pointing out some of the landmarks on the way home. While he shared news from Portland, I shared adventures, experiences, and places visited in the North.

Among those places was Lake Louise. This was the same lake that Barbi, Lois, Keith, and I had visited two years earlier. We explored its south and eastern region then, but not the northern reaches. Later, I discovered it drained into another much longer lake, which in turn drained into a remote region far to the north. This region, covering hundreds of square miles, was nearly all unsurveyed, firing my imagination. Furthermore, it was seldom visited. Only a few people I talked to knew anything about it. Studying this area over the past year, I became intrigued by its remoteness. With Dad to help paddle, I wondered how far we could push into that wild northern area.

As the fourth of July approached, Barbi, Dad, and I reached a decision to press into these backwaters. Tying Bob's twenty-foot Grumman freight canoe to the roof of the Scout, we were packing the last of our gear into the vehicle when the phone rang. Barbi's cousin Dave called us unexpectedly. His ship, the USS *Juneau* (LPD-10), had arrived in the port of Anchorage that morning. Dave was attached to the ship as a

First Lieutenant and Logistics Officer for the 2nd Battalion, 7th Marines. Asking if we were doing anything special for the weekend, he wondered if we could get together. Dampened by the thought of missing him, we told him we were pulling out of town soon and would be gone for three or four days. "Oh, that's too bad," he said. "My ship's supposed to be in port at least that long." On that, we asked if he'd like to join us.

Dave asked his ship's executive officer if he could have an extended shore leave. He explained he had relatives in Anchorage who invited him on a canoe trip a couple of hundred miles north into the wilderness. The executive officer guardedly gave his approval, with the admonition, "You make darn sure you get back here." We drove down to the shipyard to get Dave, added a few more items, and were soon on our way.

It was a bright sunny day as we pulled out of Anchorage. We did some sightseeing along the way. When we arrived at the lake, the day was getting late. Pulling into the Evergreen Lodge, we asked if we could park the Scout on their property while we were in the backwaters. They graciously consented. Hurriedly unloading our stuff, we prepared to shove off up country. In the process, though, we discovered that we were missing a fourth PFD or life jacket, as some call it.

Barbi walked back up to the lodge to ask if she could borrow one from the owners. An older fellow was there. "Sure, no problem," he said. Walking back to the waterfront with the gentleman, Barbi could hear Dave and me talking.

"Aw, I don't need one," he argued. The man walking with Barbi overheard these last few words.

Quipping to Dave matter-of-factly, he shot back, "You're probably right. You won't have long to live in those frigid waters if you go overboard." I looked up at him with a frown, wondering what he was leading up to as he continued, "However, your loved ones will be mighty happy you're wearing one 'cause it'll make it a whole lot easier for them to find your body." With that, Dave accepted the PFD that the gentleman extended. His words put a note of warning on our plans.

Quickly we finished loading the canoe and shoved off onto the lake. In the canoe were the four of us, all of our camping gear, including the wheelchair folded and tied down, several firearms and our three dogs. The dogs had been trained from early on to sit or lie down in the canoe. Although we were heavily loaded, the canoe, rated to carry one thousand eight hundred pounds, was under-loaded.

We shot across the lake to a landfall where we let the dogs out to run along the shore as we paddled north. To them, running the shore was the best part of the trip. When the brush would become too thick, they took to the water, swimming until they could run on the shore once again.

With evening approaching, we paddled along the shore until we found a suitable place to put up camp. The dogs ranged around the perimeter checking out the smells and sounds. Bugs of all kinds were honing their radar on our position, preparing to mount a full-scale attack. Someone hastily built a fire to smoke them away. The rest of us were unloading gear and establishing a campsite. Since it didn't get dark, even at night that time of the year, we had plenty of daylight, even though it was getting late into the evening. By now, Barbi had mastered cooking over an open fire. When the wood burned down to cooking coals, she had food ready to place on the fire. We ate supper at perhaps 10:00 or 11:00, and then turned in for the night.

During the following days, we explored the country, but didn't get as far north as I had hoped we would. We could see that a storm was building and didn't want to be trapped up country waiting for it to pass.

Understandably, cousin Dave was adamant about getting back to his ship on time.

One night, we sat in camp after supper, quietly visiting, as the campfire smoke drifted about us. The dogs lay close to the fire with a blanket of smoke hovering over them. Reclining and listening to the evening sounds around us, we spotted a moose about a hundred yards away. Immediately we sat up to watch her massive bulk shadow the distant backdrop. She meandered along the lake bank, cautiously approaching our camp. Occasionally she lowered her head into the water, browsing off the bottom of the lake, ten to twenty feet from the shore.

Her advance seemed somewhat unnatural, as she closed the distance between us. Although she was suspicious, she was obviously not threatened by our presence. The evening air cooled, and the wind died down making the lake surface smooth. Then the dogs saw her. They stood and shook their coats, debugging themselves, curiously watching. In a hushed voice, I told them to stay. Slowly they dropped to the ground, ears perked and alert to her approach. Warily, she gained on us continuing to browse the bottom. She was about fifty feet from where we sat spellbound. The lake surface was about halfway up her shoulders, and when her massive head lifted above the water, the fur on her neck and head seemed to liquefy as though she were melting back into the water.

Each time she submerged her head, even her ears disappeared, and she would linger submerged for close to a full minute. It became apparent that she frequented this place and believed these offshore waters belonged to her. Consequently, she wasn't about to be put out by a few strangers.

Fascinated, we decided to try and capture it on film. So the next time she dropped her head into the water, we scrambled for our cameras.

When she raised her head again, we froze. She paused, blinking with the realization that we had moved. Studying our camp momentarily, she went back to her browsing, not the least bit concerned. For twenty minutes, she lingered feeding off the bottom. Snapping pictures, it almost seemed as though she was posing for our cameras, amused by our interest. Gradually she moved out of sight.

That evening the air took on a heavy feel. Across the lake, we could see cloud layers building. Surmising the storm we anticipated brewing just beyond the horizon, we turned in for the night. Embers glowed from the campfire, as I began to play "Shenandoah," an old favorite of mine. Music haunted the lake and drifted into the silence of the forest. The harmonic sounds of the wilderness resonated with my music, as the fabric of my soul mingled with those surroundings. Settings like this comforted me from the constant reminder that I felt incomplete around those who only saw my chair. Silently, the wonder of the land settled over us. Even the wilderness didn't really fill the gaping inner wound I carried. Neither did it provide answers as to why I was forced to live in a wheelchair. In stoic silence, the land of the midnight sun reigned indifferent to my longings.

Early on the morning of our last day, the big storm we expected materialized with a nest of black clouds building in the east. Birds, normally active that time of the day, disappeared into the dark fringe of the forest. By mid-morning, bad weather began foisting itself in a fury. We watched for a lull, wanting to get up the lake and home. Clouds grew heavier, though, while the winds steadily increased. Lake Louise is a large round lake and when the wind blows, it doesn't take long to whip waves into white caps.

As we pushed off in the canoe, easterly winds were driving across our portside. Strong gusts broad-siding a heavily laden canoe in high water does not make a good combination.

Rounding a point of land, we fought against the side waves and gusty wind, as we forced our way south. These waves were larger in the open water, causing the canoe to roll sideways each time they passed under us. Then the canoe would abruptly rise two or three feet as if the lake were trying to spew us out, only to be dropped in the trough between waves as if it would then swallow us up. In between the waves, the shoreline momentarily disappeared from sight. Closer to shore, the groundswells rolled back toward us, colliding with the waves rolling from the open lake. The choppy water made it difficult to keep close to shore and run the dogs. With only six inches of freeboard, we shipped water under the crosswind. Doubtlessly, we needed to change tactics.

Dad had taken great care, teaching me to use a canoe when I was a child. When I was five, he built a canvas-covered canoe with me right by his side, fascinated with how it went together. It was a lake canoe with a deep keel. He gave me small jobs, making me feel like I really helped him build it. When finished, he patiently taught me to handle it on the big rivers and lakes. One method he used was to have me sit in the stern, paddling and steering the canoe as we trolled for fish. It took skill to keep the lines from tangling behind us, but I often tangled them.

To guide me in a straight direction, he turned around to face me in the bow. "Look over my head and pick a tree or rock on a landfall ahead of us. Do you see something you can pick out?"

"Yes!" I eagerly replied, "I see an old dead snag leaning over the water!" As a child, I was eager to meet with his approval.

"Okay, line my head up with that old snag, and don't let my head drift off to the right or left of your goal."

Of course I would drift off course, but he would say, "That's okay. Pull the bow around and line it up again. I know it's hard, but you'll get it. Stick with it."

I gradually learned to line my sight on him and stick with the goal far out on my horizon. What a wonderful lesson. As an adult, I looked to my dad and filtered my goals in life by how he might line up with them.

Thunder brought my mind back to Lake Louise. Toiling under the wind, we made slow progress. So pulling into shore, we collected the dogs and discussed our situation. Dad listened. He no longer needed to encourage me to persevere in the face of difficulty.

Waves smashing against the shore continued to build. I knew of a few islands more than a mile from where we were landed, and suggested that we might ply a course out to one of them and then shoot back south to the mainland. This meant paddling into the wind toward the islands for the first leg of the course. The advantage it would offer to us was that we could eliminate the dangerous side roll and ship less water. On the longer southwesterly leg to the mainland, we could clip along with our backs to the wind, making better time. Dad was in the bow followed by Dave, Barbi, and me in the stern. The rain was soaking our gear and us. All weary of fighting the side roll and the slow progress, we were ready for a change. Silently contemplating the risk for a few moments, we mutually agreed.

"Let's do it!" Dave shouted above the wind. Loading the dogs into the canoe, we told them to stay. In the open water, they cowered in the bottom sensing the danger. Under full stroke, we plowed toward the islands that were partly shrouded by rain and low-flying clouds.

Waves collided into the bow of the canoe, throwing a shower of water upon us, as we fought our way across the lake. The canoe rose on the first wave and then dipped steeply into the following trough. As the next wave hit the bow, wind spewed a foamy spray of water down the length of the canoe, while torrents of rain continued to shower us. All four of us strained hard into the paddles. The muscles in my shoulders and neck began to sear with hot pain, despite the cold rain assailing me. Nobody dared let up, for the unrelenting wind would treacherously turn us broadside, making us vulnerable to capsizing. It seemed as though we weren't gaining any distance, so I just bowed my back into the paddle and pulled toward the islands, lining one in particular over Dad's head. Periodically looking up to hold a steady course, I could see we were indeed making headway.

As I strained into the wind, my mind drifted back to the week when I broke my back. Red and I had asked my folks to drop us off ninety miles from home near Timothy Lake, a high mountain lake in the Cascade Mountains. We spent a week alone on the shore of that lake. Part of our gear was a canoe that Dad and I had rebuilt four years earlier. On one occasion during the week, we crossed the lake into a small bay, spending the day poking around and studying the country.

A wind had started to blow up midday, but, acting like normal sixteen-year-olds, we chose to ignore it. The little bay where we dawdled was sheltered and fairly calm. As late afternoon approached, we could tell the wind was really gusting on the main lake. When we finally left the bay, we were blasted by a fierce evening squall that whipped the lake into a white-capped frenzy. Turning the canoe back into the bay, Red asked, "What are we doing?"

Beaching the canoe, I began stripping to my skivvies. "We're going to have to paddle straight into the wind for a mile across this lake until we can reach the leeward shore." Tucking my clothes into the bow, I went on, "I don't want to get my clothes wet." That sounded like something a mountain man might do, so he followed my lead.

Back on the lake, the canoe bow smashed into the first wave and soaked my face, sending water down my chest. I blinked my eyes while shaking my head to see. Our young muscles rippled under soaked skin, as we pulled the distance across that lake for perhaps half an hour. My throat felt as dry as a ten-year-old cow chip, as we bent hard into the paddles, fighting the wind. The trip across was horrific, and my muscles seared with pain, as we slipped into the calmer leeward water. Then we sat up straight and relaxed while approaching the shore. Nosing the canoe into the sand, we heaved it to dry land. We were two very wet and beat puppies. Collapsing to the ground, we groaned from the agony that raced through our bodies. After gulping down some water, we dressed and began to recount the adventure we had made across that lake. Following the leeward shore, we returned back to our camp.

Thunder barked off in the distance, shattering my reflection of that earlier day. I could see we were almost into the leeward side of the first little island. Skimming into the protected waters, we let the dogs out and drained water from the canoe. Sparse tree cover on the island gave us shelter from the storm's blast. The rain lashed against the windward side of the island, enraging the treetops.

Then after a brief rest, we shoved out with the wind over our shoulders, pushing us toward the mainland. An abandoned cinderblock cabin lay close to its shore, and I steered us toward where I knew it to be. The canoe, driven by the wind combined with our efforts, furiously slapped against wave after wave, as we plowed forward. As the cabin came into view, I mused over the years I'd spent canoeing various backwaters. I swelled with pride. I was humbled to have a father upon whom I could still sight my goals. Moreover, I was honored that he was in agreement with the hard drive we were making toward the distant shoreline.

As we approached shore, rain pounded us even harder. The ground swells rose violently against us, causing us to ship a lot of water. Everyone else was kneeling, but I sat cross-legged in the bottom. My backside became wet and cold from the water we shipped into the canoe.

Touching shore, Dad jumped from the canoe, hooking a hand into the bow. Dave jumped from the other side, grabbing a thwart. Together they beached the canoe. Dave grabbed my chair and ran for the cabin with Barbi a few steps behind him. Dad waded out to the stern where I hooked an arm around his neck. Hoisting me up, he literally carried me in a dash for the cabin. The rain was now viciously lashing its fury upon the landscape, racing in sheets of water across the lake.

As we entered the abandoned cabin, Dad put me down easy into my chair and walked to the window. There was no glass in the windows, nor a door on the hinges of that old cinderblock cabin, but we still huddled under its roof, although I'm not sure why. Soaked to the bone, I sat in a soaked chair. Rivulets of water drove across that old floor. The wind howled, reaching through the door and windows, as if to snatch us in its cruel grip and hurl us across the taiga in bitter retribution for our trespassing into this untamed land. It felt colder inside than it did outside. Barbi shuddered. Still, nobody ventured outdoors. The rain lashed into the one-room cabin through the eastern window, hammering the floor and nearby wall. The force became deafening, and we shouted to each other above the din. Despite all this, we smiled over our narrow escape. Finally the storm exhausted its force, reducing its ferocity to a gentle roar.

Once more, I had a feeling of satisfaction, reflecting on the harrowing experience we had managed to live through. Events like these proved to me that feelings of inadequacy were sometimes wrong ideas. Ideas have consequences. Through time, they can paralyze the heart. We faced a challenge that didn't allow for even the slightest error. That was a wild ride, and we could have easily met with a watery grave.

All these years later, I still recall Dad looking at me when the storm quieted down and asking, "Did that frighten you?"

For a long moment, not wanting to admit that it might have killed us, I mulled it over. Then looking up with a gleam in my eye, I quietly replied, "Not too much."

While I didn't recognize it at the time, how often I have learned since those years, the wisdom of plying a course with my heavenly Father in the helm of life's ship. With God before us, who can stand against us? It was God who did not spare His own Son, but delivered Him up for us all. I have become convinced over many years that nothing, not any storm of life, can separate us from the love of God that we have in Christ Jesus. When those angry groundswells of life sweep over us, we have a Father that turned His world upside down to get into our boat, face us, and guide us to our destination. And when the time comes, He will one day hook into our boat and carry us into our heavenly home with the admonition, "Do not fear, for I am with you."

The rest of the trip back to the Evergreen Lodge was uneventful, and the rain almost ceased. The storm had unveiled its worst moment, and what followed was child's play. The wind did howl around a few more headlands, however, before we pulled into the lodge. Cousin Dave made it back to his ship according to schedule and departed soon thereafter. As Dad wrapped up his trip and returned home, I found myself deeply thankful that he had sacrificed his time to come to Alaska and be with us.

In the fall, when the birds began the Zugunruhe, I mentioned to Barbi that I was going to drive down onto the Kenai Peninsula, take a canoe up the Moose River, and go moose hunting. Flying over this country before we were married, I became captivated by its nearly impenetrable mosaic of taiga and muskeg.

She passively replied, "Who's going with you?"

"There's nobody to go with, so I'm going alone."

Instantly she raised her head, giving me far more attention than I wanted. She didn't like the idea of me canoeing into that wilderness country alone one little bit. "What if you get hurt?" she blurted.

"What if I got hurt anywhere else?" I shot back, reflecting how irrelevant I thought her question was. We proceeded to clash about it into the evening. Weeks away, I couldn't see getting worked up over it then, so I let it go. When the time came, I was sure to have my way, and she'd have to drop it.

The venture of undertaking the journey alone in that uninhabited region appealed to me. Deep down inside, I harbored a desire to conquer my sense of being un-whole as a man. I needed to prove something. Taking this trip alone held distinct power in my mind.

However, she kept bringing it up from time to time and wouldn't let it ride. As the time grew near, the issue came up again. Still alarmed, she offered, "If you haven't found anyone to go with you yet, I'd really like to go with you."

I didn't mind if she went, but I craved the challenge of going alone. Try as I might, I couldn't seem to raise the importance of this need above her protest. Safety was her utmost concern. Over the next several days, she mentioned it to various friends, and they agreed with her. Armed with their support, she became more adamant.

Mere days remained as she railed on, throwing out every reason she could conjure to keep me from hunting alone. By that time, she had worked herself into a widow whose husband had disappeared in the bush, his body never found. Gradually, for her peace of mind, I considered letting her come with me. Barbi had never been hunting before, and I wasn't sure how she would respond to gutting and field dressing a moose and packing it out in the canoe. The rigors of the hunt would make it more than just a camping trip.

Eventually I caved in to her concern. "Okay, but you've got to be quiet and not complain." Telling her not to complain was added more to emphasize my objection than to issue a warning. Barbi was really not one to complain about anything. However, the jury was out on how *quiet* she'd be.

She brightened up immediately. I think it was more because she was going on an adventure with me than because she had won the battle. She really enjoyed our adventures together. One of the many things that drew me to her was her eagerness to join in my rough and sometimes primitive pursuits. After all, I reckoned, how many beautiful and intelligent professional women would abandon their cosmopolitan lifestyle in civilized surroundings to travel into the frontier of Alaska to be with the man she loved?

Although I was a little torqued that I wouldn't reach my goal of going alone, I secretly admired her pluck. Still, I made it a point to show her that I could do this without any help.

When we arrived at the quiet little boat landing on the Moose River, I told her to stand aside, as I stormed about in a suitable fashion, unloading the canoe from the Scout and transferring our gear and my chair into it. I was proving it to myself as much as to Barbi. I needed to know that my wheelchair did not hold me back, and I could indeed do this thing without any help. When I was ready, I sat in the stern, shoved off, and swung the bow back into the shore. Grounding the canoe, I invited her to jump in.

She beamed with the smile that drove me to call her Sunshine. Then she reiterated, "I have no doubt that you're physically capable of going up river on your own. I just didn't believe it was safe for you to go alone." I loved her for that note of confidence. Her words put substance to the intangible satisfaction I hoped to gain from the wilderness. She jumped into the front seat of the canoe facing toward the bow.

Seated in the stern, I smiled at my bride who radiated happiness, even with her back to me. Rifle leaning against a thwart, we struck off from our launch site. Immediately Barbi wanted to visit. Despite my warning, she thought we were going to have a wonderful time visiting for several days and became surprised when I told her we had to be very *quiet*. Slipping quietly upstream, we pulled against a gentle current.

Rounding a bend in the river, civilization slipped behind us. The shoreline drifted past, while I searched for sign of moose.

Soon Barbi became weary of the silence and wanted to visit in whispers. Being on a gentle reach of the river, every sound, including the noise from the canoe amplified through the forest. Softly, I reminded her that we needed to be aware of every sound we made, or we'd alert everything within earshot of our presence.

When we met, she was no stranger to a canoe. She had canoed Puget Sound with the Girl Scouts in some rough water, I might add. Nevertheless, she habitually bumped the paddle on the side of the canoe on her backstroke. In the stillness of that meandering river, the paddle striking the aluminum canoe seemed to echo in every direction. "Watch your backstroke," I whispered. She fussed back at me that she was trying to be quiet.

Indeed, I knew she was, but the canoe hull drove the sound up and down the river. Chewing over her response, I thought, *Okay, take a deep breath. When we round the next bend, we'll try again.*

The farther up the river we traveled, the more the tyranny of silence tormented her and made her uncomfortable. Then her paddle dropped across the gunwales of the canoe echoing through the aluminum. Over her shoulder, she insouciantly whispered, "Sorry." With her hands free, she begin to fidget, trying to make herself comfortable.

Again, I gently pleaded, "Shh... We've got to be very quiet."

Intensity rose in her voice, as she shot back, "I'm trying to, but this thing's jabbing me." Pulling at a pack, she dislodged an avalanche of supplies into the bottom of the canoe. Then, grabbing the paddle, she splashed it into the water like a beaver's tail sounding off an alarm.

"Dip your paddle into the water gently like I'm doing, so it doesn't splash," I softly encouraged. Facing forward, she couldn't see my expression. My words alone sounded like fault-finding imperatives. I backed off, as her shoulders stiffened. In my short years of marriage, I had acquired much expertise in getting my red-haired bride upset.

Around the next bend, she softly laid the paddle down and quietly dug down deep into her pack. I wondered what she was doing. A bird fluttered down the river so quietly I could hear its wings pulsing through the air. An almost imperceptible breeze drifted past us. Surrounded by excellent moose habitat, I was sure we might see one. Then suddenly Barbi's hand emerged from her pack with a candy bar. Its wrapper, objecting to a full-scale attack, broke the silence of the afternoon. My shoulders dropped. Bit by bit, I saw that penetrating this primitive wasteland would challenge me in a way I'd never imagined. Again I hushed a low "Shh...." Sheepishly looking back over her shoulder, she tried *quietly* to wrestle the candy from the wrapper.

These things repeated themselves on into the evening until we spotted a fine-looking campsite on top of the riverbank. Pulling close to the bank, I mulled over a way to get out while the canoe floated in the water. Tasks that were otherwise simple to the average person often frustrated me with complications. The river was deep at this location and the bank dropped two or three feet vertically into the water. Tying the canoe to some stout roots in the bank, we let the current point it downstream. I tossed my chair on the bank and gently rose, sitting on the stern. Without my legs, it was tricky to avoid hurting myself or taking a bath. The canoe wobbled but held fast, as I hoisted onto the riverbank. From there, it was an easy lift into the chair.

While the late afternoon cool air subdued the mosquitoes that time of the year, the *no see 'ums* were out in hordes. I dressed with thick heavy clothing to protect myself from these nearly invisible flies and then ignored them around my face. Barbi on the other hand, waged a personal vendetta against these pesky biting flies, and there wasn't much of a chance to hunt around camp that evening.

Barbi had become a talented campfire cook by this time. She planned a much better meal than my ordinary hamburger stew. Supper was delicious and offset the arduous strained silence we had worked through that day. We enjoyed the coolness of the night, as the sun went down, taking the bugs with it. My joy in having her with me consumed my desire for being alone. The river silently flowed along as we sat on the bank, visiting into the evening. Enveloped by the coming darkness and the satisfying stillness, I felt at peace. Starlight danced on the water that slipped its way to the sea, while the firelight flickered in the darkness. Although conquering this venture alone would have been rewarding, it couldn't have been as satisfying. While I craved the lonely freedom the serene wilderness offered, the woman at my side made me complete. In the tranquility of that moment, time stood still, as her warmth pressed against me. We gradually grew quiet. Contemplating my blessing, I had a treasure few other men allow themselves to know.

The next morning, we slipped out early, pursuing a course toward the head of the river. When we packed the gear this time, however, we put the wheelchair in the bottom of the canoe, covering it with our gear. The events of the day before repeated themselves in tormented silence, as Barbi tried to occupy herself with various things to keep her peace in the canoe. I began to give up the idea of hunting, amusing myself by watching her *try* to be quiet. Up river, we encountered several small riffles. Pushing through them, we dragged the bottom of the canoe on the rocks. The river current became stronger in places, taking more work to continue upstream. I halfheartedly hunted, but the noise in the canoe and the battle against the river stole most of our attention.

Pressing upstream, Barbi became more captivated by what might lie around the next bend. Finally, we encountered a rapid that we couldn't get past. It looked like the end of the line. We could see slack water just beyond the rapid and farther still lay another bend. The hunt, long since forsaken, took second precedence to exploring this country.

Barbi turned in the seat and said, "I think we could get past this rapid if I get out and pull the canoe." This was one of the real crippling effects I struggled against in my mind. I was more than a little chagrined at the prospect of her pulling the canoe with me sitting in it. Her eagerness to press on was contagious, but the idea really bit hard. She jumped out of the canoe, and the bow immediately rose above the rocks. Grabbing the bow line, she started pulling before I had much to say. "See, I can pull, and it won't be that bad."

Struggling with my sense of identity, I poled against the bottom with the paddle. We skirted around a few more bends after that, but my wings felt clipped. I silently mulled over my inability to do something as simple as step out of a canoe. Once again my thoughts echoed in the hollow abyss that threatened to consume me. Approaching another shallow rapid, Barbi again jumped out to pull, but this time my dead weight put a greater drag in the stern. Even so, she put her shoulder into the rope until we ground to a halt.

Spiraling downward, my mind pulled me into that hollow place without answers. My crippled body held my attitude hostage to my circumstances, causing me to nurse my misfortune. This *wasn't* why I came out here. Water washed beneath the bow, as incompetence washed away my ability to reason.

Calling it self-pity or pride eclipses the greater need. Suffering a terrible loss creates an agony that exceeds pity. It's genuine grief that only time and understanding can attend. Mired in this train of thought, all I could think to do was the very thing I couldn't accomplish: get out and pull my own load. Old irresolvable feelings began to take control.

Echoing from many years before, words from my childhood came back to me: 'Your bed may have been made for you, but you don't have to sleep in it.' I thought *don't let your misfortune define your destiny. Abandon the idea that you can't and get out of the bed that's mired your thoughts. Don't dwell on your circumstances; overcome them.* These thoughts gave me the means to escape my attitude of inadequacy and self-loathing that contributed nothing toward our goal. I struggled to suppress those negative feelings so I could think objectively. If we could relieve my weight from the canoe through another fifty feet of shallow rapids, we'd be in deep water again.

Emerging from that dark realm within, a thought struck me. If I took a paddle into each hand and pushed them into the riverbed, I might use them as a person uses crutches to get off a couch. In that, I could lift myself up and eliminate most of my weight. Trying this, the canoe rose up, so that Barbi was able to easily drag it forward. When the paddles passed beyond my center of gravity, I dropped my weight back to the bottom of the canoe. Several times I repeated the act. It didn't resolve my inward struggle, but it met the immediate need.

We did this successfully several times when I began to see a rustling in the shoulder high grass along the opposite bank of the river. The water churning across the rapids had masked all sound. Still alert to the possibility of a moose, however, this movement captured my attention. Deftly pulling the paddles into the canoe, I reached for my rifle. Then I saw the heads of two men and two women bouncing just over the top of the grass beyond the small rise. They were headed our way and hadn't seen us yet. Furthermore, Barbi hadn't seen them.

This was really going to be embarrassing. There I sat, utterly helpless in the canoe, while Barbi pulled it through the rapids. Swept with a whole new sense of melancholy, I remembered the wheelchair was buried in the bottom of the canoe. I tried to imagine how this looked: a small-framed woman pulling a healthy young man sitting in a freight canoe. I winced.

There are times when being crippled can make a guy feel awfully compromised. But there was nothing that could be done about it. Just before the four hikers crested the hill to see us, a thought struck me. Instantly, my melancholy lifted. Folding my arms across my chest, I protruded my elbows outward. Acting like the sheik of the North, flying through the air on a magic carpet, I commanded the scene. I assumed a stern countenance and sat there fixing a hard stare at Barbi. Really, I wasn't going to be able to do anything anyway, so I just acted like this was all normal, oblivious to the group crowning the rise. Why not make the best of it!

The hikers had been focused on the natural beauty sweeping out before them. On gaining the high ground, however, the hill broke off to the river below. In the middle of all that grandeur, they saw us, as unexpected as a pig in a wedding. We undoubtedly presented one of the most outlandish scenes they ever witnessed in their entire lives. Seated in the canoe cross-legged, elbows extended outward, I acted like walking was above my dignity. My rifle rested across my lap; its barrel set between the thwart and gunnel of that twenty-foot Grumman canoe.

Still not aware of the present invasion, Barbi hunkered harder under the sudden drag. Sensing the weight was no longer being intermittently relieved from the canoe, she stopped breathlessly and turned toward me with a puzzled frown. Sitting in my sheik pose, she was momentarily swept away with a most bewildered look. It was then she caught movement on the hill out of the corner of her eyes. The guys elbowed the gals and were pointing at her! Those poor women, hands cupped to their faces, were aghast in stunned horror at what they were witnessing.

To those backpackers, we must have made a scene to which the grandeur of the Alaskan wilderness couldn't compete. Above the din of the rapids, we couldn't hear a word they were saying, but their gestures said it all. Barbi's eyes went from them to me and back again. It gradually dawned on her that I was clowning around. Discovering themselves the subject of our intense investigation, the gals hastily turned their companions off that ridge and disappeared. Perhaps they wanted to avoid an unpleasant encounter with the denizens of that sometimes-lawless country.

After they vanished, I started laughing, wondering how much weight those women carried in their packs after that. Fortunately for me, they disappeared before Barbi came out of her astounded shock. Dropping the rope, she began fighting the rapids and rock-strewn river bottom to come at me, waving a paddle. I instantly experienced a new kind of helplessness, but this time it was from not being able to escape my red-haired fury. Presently, however, we ended up laughing uncontrollably. We have laughed more over that incident than perhaps any other event in our marriage.

My battle to overcome wilderness obstacles was nearly as problematic in my mind as it was on the ground. Adaptations could be accomplished when I kept a clear mind. Barbi's confidence in me paved the way for such clear thinking. My battle against those who only saw a wheelchair persisted, though, while my career potential widened.

CHAPTER ELEVEN

On a Career Path

Fighting against naysayers, the education I gained over the previous three years had placed me in a more competitive position as a land law examiner. Supervisory responsibilities advanced me on the pay scale. Although passionate about living in Alaska, I knew if I wanted to advance to a job with outdoor field responsibilities I would have to leave the state. To do that, I needed to solicit help at the highest BLM level in Alaska. These managers knew me and were confident that I could handle a field job.

I approached the BLM state director in Alaska during the late spring of 1978 and asked for his assistance in helping me find a position in the lower 48. He initiated letters to each of the eleven western states where the BLM had a prominent presence. The letters described my situation and asked them to determine if there were any field jobs I might qualify for. Afterward, there was a long and expected lull in my search. For a period of time, it seemed to languish.

Overall, it rained much more than normal that summer, causing our potatoes to rot in the ground. When it wasn't raining, the skies seemed to be continuously cloudy. The rain was making both of us restless, driving us to travel inland just to see some blue skies. Wanting to move to a location with much less rain, I kept wondering what was happening with the letters sent out a few months earlier. That summer, I also applied for a position as a realty specialist at the Phoenix Training Center in Arizona. The training center had a Land School program to train men and women in a two-month course to become realty specialists at various field stations. These people were sent into remote areas to determine the environmental effects of proposals to use public lands. After a short waiting period, I received a notice of rejection with no explanation. While I was disappointed, I still had an ace in the hole with the state director's letters, so I continued waiting.

During the late summer, the Land Office in Fairbanks needed interim help in a vacated branch chief position. This was an opportunity to gain experience managing an office, and I left to fill the position for a total of ten or twelve weeks. Barbi had a cadre of family visiting, so she was going to have her hands full with company.

As fall approached, I became settled into a routine, running the branch. One day someone asked if I'd assist in an effort to promote the smoke jumpers in the BLM's firefighting program. These were considered among the bravest firefighters in the country. The BLM intended to feature their work in a promotional recruitment film.

Sounding like a good break from the daily routine, I met the crew out on the tarmac late that afternoon. Two planes were involved in this effort. The BLM smoke jumpers in the first plane would be filmed from a second, with the photographer leaning out the cargo door at the end of a tether. They had tried the whole operation once before, but the photographer couldn't hear communications above the noise of the howling wind and plane's engines. They needed someone in the second plane to communicate between the pilot and the photographer. That's were I came into the picture. Having flown with the BLM, I knew the flight protocol and felt comfortable lending a hand—that is, until I reached the plane.

The plane I was to fly in stood quietly on the tarmac a hundred yards away, waiting while we went through a short briefing. Bob, the photographer, was the same guy who had helped me build a ramp to my trailer five years earlier. We were good friends and worked well together. He did enjoy a practical joke at times though. Hustling out to the plane, as I rounded the tail I saw the cargo door was removed. Craning to see inside the plane, I spied only one seat. It was for the pilot. Butterflies started stirring the pit of my stomach.

"You don't want me to sit in my chair in the plane, do you?" The words just spontaneously popped out of my mouth. Visions of rolling out the door raged in my mind.

Reaching around through the opening, Bob produced a seatbelt attached to a puny nylon tether that dangled in the air. Holding it up with a measured smile, he said, "You'll be sitting on the floor anywhere you want to. Just clip the end down over there." He pointed to a place in the bulwark of the plane. "Of course if you're worried about it, or think you can't do it, I guess we can get someone else. But that will sure slow us down."

Believing he was kidding me, I peered into the back of the plane for a seat of some kind. Nothing. I had marginal trust in my chair, but I held no trust for an airplane without a seat or a door. The pilot walked up and climbed into the plane. The other plane's pilot started its engines and smoke jumpers were filing out toward it. I looked back at Bob who stood there with a twinkle in his eye.

Our pilot started the plane's engines and checked the instrument panel. Apparently I must have been hesitating because Bob interrupted my thoughts with, "What do you want to do?" Jumping into a situation I lacked even marginal confidence in stretched me. I felt in the grip of sudden death.

Wavering, I mulled *who would ask someone to go on a plane ride and forget to mention that there wasn't a seat or a door on the plane!*

The last of the smoke jumpers were gathering at the door of their plane, and our pilot turned and shouted over the noise of the engines, "Get in!" Preparing to help out on a mission with some of America's bravest, I stared into the empty hollow of a plane, aware that I had no parachute. Gulping hard, I shrugged. I wasn't about to reveal any doubt about my own courage. If a couple of hundred feet over a cliff in a car didn't kill me, a thousand five hundred feet from an airplane would. *Buck up!* I thought, swinging from my chair to the deck. Then I scooted across the floor.

Seatbelt secure around my waist, I tethered the strap into the bulwark. I couldn't help but wonder about the risks. Bob, seatbelt secure around his waist, grabbed my chair and shoved it toward the hangar. The loose end of his tether dangled at his side. The moment that chair disappeared, a sudden need to urinate seized me. Bob quickly returned, jumped in through the opening still smiling, and then connected his tether into a different point in the bulwark.

My imagination went wild. It seemed as though the opening in the fuselage suddenly grew larger. *Okay, Bob,* I pondered, *he who laughs first doesn't always laugh last.* Immediately we were taxiing down the runway. Concrete speeding directly underneath my nose reminded me of the tether. I noticed I had a death grip on it. *Relax boy,* I implored myself, loosening my grip, but just a little. *This probably won't kill you.* Glancing at my fingers, it looked like I'd squeezed the blood out of them.

Lifting off behind the first plane, I watched an old familiar sight of trees and muskeg diminish in size below me. However, it seemed as though I had never experienced it before. All of my attention focused on the opening when the pilot's voice came across my headset. "Can you read me, Dave?"

Startled, I jumped at his voice. "Loud and clear," I said through the headset, trying to look composed.

"Are you okay?" he quizzed.

"Sure," I shot back. That's when I noticed how thirsty I was. I really wished I'd brought some water along on this trip. Bob sat near the opening, camera in hand. I was plastered to the opposite side. The smoke jumpers' plane emerged to the right and ahead of us. I actually relaxed and let go of the tether. Bereft of the use of my legs, I felt if we hit any turbulence, I was going to turn into a human yoyo.

All at once things began to happen. We were approaching the drop zone, and everyone positioned for the maneuver. Bob told me to scoot over toward the door, so he could see my signals. Near the door, the wind pulled at my shirt. Then the pilot came across my headset, notifying me we were making another pass. I communicated to Bob using hand signals, alerting him that we were making a new approach. Subsequently, both planes made a wide sweeping turn to the right. The door side of the plane dipped toward the ground reducing the visibility through the door to one-third sky and two-thirds Earth. I wanted to holler, 'Turn left! Turn left!' Preparing to slide out of the plane, my hand shot back to the tether. To my amazement, though, I didn't slide an inch. Instead, I just leaned into the turn.

We made another approach, this time with success. Bob's camera went into action, while I communicated from the pilot to Bob with hand signals. As Bob slightly leaned out the opening, his hair whipped about while the wind tore at his clothing. His tether was tight. I watched with amazement at the daring skill demonstrated by those smoke jumpers, as one by one, in immediate succession, they bailed out of their plane. Instantly, a realization hit me: my role was perhaps the safest, most miniscule position in the effort, yet without my participation, the entire mission would have failed to get off the ground.

Everything clicked off as planned, and the job soon ended. We continued on a northerly course, as the first plane circled south toward the landing field. After a few minutes, the jump plane made a sharp bank again to the right, and we followed. With this turn, the horizon almost completely disappeared from my view out the door. Although it was a little unnerving, I started to feel like I was wearing that plane. Again I leaned into it. At 175 mph, the centrifugal force, combined with the tether, held me in place. I didn't feel nearly as vulnerable as I had earlier.

Bob had his back to the inside wall of the fuselage, and we both watched out the door. The rush of air and the roar of the engines eliminated any verbal communication. Bob pointed to a moose below us. The muskeg tundra of the boreal forest rushed below. Intermittently, sunlight flashed silvery threads off the labyrinth of tiny waterways that flowed through the marshy muskeg, as we raced for home. We made our final bank to the right and were soon on the ground.

I've often thought of the tether that was the only real connection between that airplane and me. It clipped solidly to the plane but seemed a meager connection. That tether is very much like faith. I may have a seatbelt around my waist, yet allow my tether to dangle at my side. Faith means discovering what I'm called to do and connecting to it.

We didn't take time for a honeymoon after our wedding, because we needed to be back to work. We often talked about taking one later. So as our third anniversary rolled around, I returned from Fairbanks, and we booked a passage on a ferry destined for Kodiak Island. Our scheduled departure from Seward was on the M/V *Tustumena*, a 296-foot vessel owned and operated by the Alaska Marine Highway System. We arrived at the ferry early on a morning that, from the town of Seward, looked like a beautiful clear day. After we drove below deck, a crewmember guided us to a designated spot. As we exited the Scout, we told the dogs to behave and locked them in the vehicle with the windows partly opened.

As we walked away from the vehicle, we saw a seaman hustling toward us, carrying some large shackles. Without saying a word, he dropped to the deck, slid under the Scout, and hooked the shackles to the axles and then into concealed anchor points just under the surface of the deck.

"Why's he doing that?" Barbi asked.

We had traveled on a few Alaska ferries, and I couldn't remember anyone doing that before. Other crewmembers hustled to do the same thing to the remaining trucks and cars nearby.

"Well, I guess they're securing their load, so it doesn't shift," I pondered aloud. If I'd completely thought my response to its final conclusion, I would have begun babbling to the crew to put us immediately off the ship. Obviously they were in a hurry, and so we shrugged, backed out of their way, and went above deck.

The day brightened with the coming sun, and the sky was a beautiful deep blue. We worked our way into the ship's cafeteria and leisurely sat down near a window, ordering coffee and breakfast. As we ate, I noticed there weren't many people on board. All considered, though, the tourist season was over, so the census would normally be low. The ship slipped its berth on schedule, and the trip out of Resurrection Bay was relaxing. The twelve-hour trip would put us in Kodiak early that evening. The southern coast of the Kenai Peninsula abounds with massive cliffs dropping into the sea with dangerous reefs scattered in the breakwaters. Travelers along this section can expect to see some of the most beautiful and rugged coasts in Alaska, teeming with wildlife.

Resurrection Bay sparkled under the early morning sunlight. A stiff breeze with a dropping temperature blew in from the gulf. After all, we could expect it to be cold. November was just around the corner. As we neared the mouth of the bay, I could see the wind whipping up the open sea and said to Barbi, "It looks like it might be a little choppy." Rounding the point and bearing southwest, however, I froze. A black wall of clouds, stretching out to sea as far as the eye could reach, shrouded the horizon. Reaching skyward, it scourged against the vault of heaven. North toward the mainland, the mountains vanished. It was so black, it looked as though we might have to cut our way into it.

Suddenly, the wind caught us a few points off the bow of the ship, causing her to heave under the strain. My mouth went dry, and a terrible feeling churned in the pit of my stomach. Looking around, I could see others examining the horizon in sober dread at the ghastly sight we were approaching. For a moment, I deceived myself into thinking that the captain, being of sound mind and thinking like me, would turn the ship around and skedaddle back to Seward. What folly men embrace in the face of unexpected storms!

As we penetrated that weather bank, a horrific storm instantly engulfed us. As the great sea tempest mounted to its ugly potential, the waves rose and fell in unspeakable fury. Dinner was announced, and I was curious to see who went to eat. The galley was nearly empty, save for a few tough and tried seamen. Barbi found a lounge chair bolted to the deck and held on tight. The ship slowed to about 6 or 7 knots, while the pilot tried to keep it near the crest of the oncoming waves. But since we were on a course tangent to the wind, the ship would eventually pitch forward and roll slightly to the side into the trough between the waves. Her propellers seemed to momentarily rise out of the water. The ship amplified their furious whine until the ship's stern slipped back into the black water, leaving us with the increasing wail and moan of the wind. Assailing rain lashed at her capriciously like claws scraping her bulkhead in an effort to pry her apart. The din of the rain and the wind was almost deafening.

Increasing in fury, it pitched and heaved the ship, whipping and rolling my chair uncontrollably. Whenever the ship dove at a steep angle to the bottom of a trough, it sent me crashing against a wall, where I scrambled to grab hold of something solid. Before I knew what hit us, an oncoming wave collided with the ship, sending a shudder through her decks. Staring through the window, I saw nothing but water pour from her topside for a span of twenty to thirty seconds. Slowly she climbed from below the onslaught wave, leaving the trough to ride a new crest. The seconds ticked by, as I openly wondered if we would re-emerge to the surface. Later I discovered that the sea swells rose between 40 and 60 feet at one point, and the wind gusts were toward 100 mph.

In the gray light of midday, through a veil of rain, we occasionally made out the form of waves driven into the cliffs with a thunderous force. The hours dragged on while my arms grew weary steadying myself against the lurching beneath my hurricane deck. My chair at times nearly careened out from under me. My weight seemed to teeter forward onto the front wheels of which I had no control, sending me headlong into a bulkhead again. Finally I took my bandanna and tied my chair to a support post anchored to the deck and hooked my arm around the back of my chair. The gathering darkness of late afternoon fell like a stone, engulfing us with a sense of helplessness to the pitching of the ship and maelstrom blast against her hull. All we could think about was the sanctuary of the safe harbor in Kodiak. Supper was announced, and I could not even imagine cooking food, let alone eating it. I stayed tied to the ship.

I first went to sea as a young boy fishing over the Columbia River bar, yet I never experienced anything like this storm. While I was tied fast, Barbi generously offered to bring me some water. Walking like a tipsy sailor, though, she returned with only a Dixie cup half full. She lay back down, again clinging to the recliner. I have ridden on many ships in Alaska, and this was the only time I completely lacked any desire to go out on the open deck and look around.

The fierce gale continued throughout the night, as the ship plunged and staggered, periodically swallowed by the effervescent turbulence of the sea. We tried to sleep where we landed earlier, but the ship's convulsions would instantly jolt us awake, forcing us to seize hold to prevent being thrown to the deck. This continued throughout the night, as our weariness converted into raggedness. Time and again, our thoughts returned to those poor dogs down in the hold.

Morning dawned with the call for breakfast, and the storm showed signs of exhausting itself. The gray gloom of the day before eventually passed, though the ship still rolled in the roiling sea. Twenty-four hours after we departed from Seward, we entered the safe harbor of Kodiak. There the water became smooth, sheltered from the brutal winds buffeting the open sea. As we pulled into the harbor, I finally went out on deck. I spotted one of the officers and stopped to visit. "That was quite the storm last night," I casually commented.

"Yeah, it wasn't the worst I've been through," he came back.

I wondered what could possibly be worse that wouldn't require the deployment of lifeboats.

There was a pause. Then after eyeing me up and down, he followed with a fascinating story of a storm they experienced the previous year. Apparently, an eighty-foot fishing vessel was caught in a similar gale. Disabled, she sent out distress signals for help. The captain of the ship we were on responded to the call. They came alongside the vessel and saved all hands just minutes before the fishing vessel went to the bottom of the sea. He said that the captain was given a citation for the rescue, referring me to a newspaper article on the wall near the purser's station.

I wandered inside to read the article. I was awed by the skill and courage of the captain and crew during that rescue. It was then that I fully appreciated the captain who had guided our ship through that storm.

Drawing a parallel from this incident at a vantage point many years later, I wonder: How often is it that folks pray for a harbor of sanctuary from life's storms, not realizing that if they know God, they are in the far better sanctuary of Jesus Christ? As mere mortals, we don't fully understand the Captain. In our human reasoning, we wonder why He doesn't turn our ship around and keep us out of life's storms. But the storms we struggle through are not beyond His power to bring us safely through them. On the other hand, living through those storms can teach us so much.

Concern for the dogs was heavy on our minds, as we returned to the Scout that morning. There was every reason to believe we would meet with a horrible mess in the vehicle. Yet to our surprise when we opened the door, the vehicle was just as we had left it. Canine smiles and furiously wagging tails greeted us. Somehow, in obedience to the mystery of nature's laws, the dogs must have entered into a brief state of aestivation. After we disembarked from the ship and vehicle, they ran through the grass joyfully expressing their relief. We gave them a long run and then found a hotel and slept half the day. That tumultuous ride continued to protract itself upon my equilibrium as I lay down. The bed seemed to pitch and fall under me long after I fell asleep.

The ferry ride home was peaceful. A brisk sea wind rose from the Gulf of Alaska, possessing a sense of impending winter. Outside on the open deck, it ripped at my clothing. The sky, cast in a deep blue, accented the fall colors of the mainland's seascape. The grandeur of the southern Kenai coast unfolded before us in magnificent splendor. Sea life teemed over the surface of the water. Tremendous waves crashed against the cliffs and reefs along the mainland, as seabirds soared overhead, ringing out their song of the sea.

The wonder of the seascape spread before me lent inner strength. The liberty to move across unfettered places partly subjugated my enslavement to paraplegia. Although I was adapting to my life on the hurricane deck, it constantly restrained me. I felt most free whenever the earth slipped easily beneath me.

CHAPTER TWELVE

Running the North's Gauntlet

Life on the move appealed to me. Travel, whether on holiday or for my job, relieved the duress I felt, due to paraplegia. I craved to be free. Simply viewed, it could be said I was running from myself. Greater, though, was my desire to escape the gaping abyss that paraplegia had sent me falling into, helplessly en route to utter anguish. It was more than simply running from something physically tangible. There was an ever-present intangible ache deep within me for which there seemed to be no swath to bind my wound.

My job led me farther from Anchorage. This travel offered limited freedom. At the same time, my job demanded more of my time in the office. These distractions presented themselves as possible avenues of escape from the emptiness bottled up inside me. These escapes, futile as they were, satisfied my immediate restlessness.

On the other hand, I had more than just myself to consider. Distractions stole time from my marriage. Art fell among those distractions. It wasn't difficult to share Alaska's frontier with Barbi, but she never seemed to be able to enter my world of art. How the colors blended to bring out shapes and forms was a complete enigma to her. When I became stirred to express my imagination on canvas, I found that if I didn't sequester myself and dedicate a large block of time to it right then, the inspiration would diminish or vanish. As was my habit, I withdrew from anything around me when occupied with my artwork. In those youthful years, I couldn't find a way to allocate time between Barbi, travel, job, and art without detracting from one or the other.

Time spent at home carried a high premium. It wasn't right retreating into my artwork when I arrived home after being gone long hours or days. I was unwilling to exclude my bride from more of my life than forced to, so I began tapering time spent on my artwork. Besides, being with her brought greater satisfaction; she meant more to me than my penchant to wander or create. Something unpretentious emanated from her, encouraging me to a greater life. It was an indiscernible strength I longed to possess.

Reduced to selling pencil or pen drawings, time spent in my business languished. Art couldn't compete with my wanderings, plus my new BLM responsibilities. As I developed new skills within the BLM, I found I had an aptitude for administrative law. Thus, I spent more time educating myself through classes at the University of Alaska, focusing on the field of real estate law. More opportunities, expanding into supervisory/managerial roles, took me deeper into my work. There was less time to dedicate to drawing pictures, and I couldn't see any economic future in it. Eventually I abandoned the business altogether.

Barbi treasured my art and was disappointed when I put my paints away. Occasionally I did a quick sketch for someone or doodled on scratch paper in my spare time. One day, I may again ply my skills onto canvas when I'm older, as life slows down for me.

Ultimately though, my goal to work outdoors drove me toward proficiency in administrative law. Through that field, I saw an avenue into a field-oriented career as a realty specialist.

On Friday after Thanksgiving in 1978, I had a message to call Jeff Steele in the BLM Riverside District Office (later, the California Desert District Office). Jeff had heard that I was looking for a job. Previous to our visit, he spoke with the state director of the BLM in Alaska who personally recommended me for the job. On the phone, I listened to Jeff describe a job he was creating in his district. The job was district realty specialist for the BLM's Withdrawal Review Program. This was a prototype nationwide program for which the BLM in California accepted the lead responsibility. In 1976, the United States Congress required the BLM to quickly get this review off the ground and finish it within a time frame of fifteen years. They allocated $10 million to do it. Typically, lands of unique or special interest were removed from settlement entry or appropriation under a variety of Washington orders. The BLM collectively referred to these orders as withdrawals. The purpose of the withdrawals was to prevent those lands from going into private ownership. The appropriation laws, including the various homestead and mining laws, had by and large been repealed, however.

Consequently, Congress questioned the need to expend money to administer the vast number of withdrawals. However, continuation of some withdrawals was necessary to prevent entry under a few remaining appropriation laws such as the Desert Land Entry Act and the 1872 Mining Law. The vast majority had no agricultural or mineral value though, thus needing no protection. In any case, they needed to be evaluated to make a final determination. Whoever was appointed to this job would need to spend a large amount of time in the field. After all was said, Jeff offered me the job hands down if I was interested. If I accepted the assignment, I would develop a prototype program in California that each state in the BLM could follow.

The program needed to be pioneered from the ground up, meaning I would need to spend a great amount of time alone on the Mojave Desert, evaluating natural resource values. I had no great desire to move to California because of the heat, but it was obvious that this was going to be my one shot to prove I could do field work from a wheelchair.

Jeff flatly stated, "This job will either allow you to write your own ticket in the BLM, or if you fail, run a desk next to a Xerox machine the rest of your career." I told him I'd talk it over with my wife and let him know on Monday.

The hard part was going to be convincing my bride that she *wanted* to live in the Southwest. Barbi really liked living a life of adventure in Alaska. I needed to convince her that moving could be a great adventure as well as the fulfillment of a dream. Driving down Arctic Boulevard, I rehearsed in my mind how I might convince her to move from Alaska; I well recalled her aversion to the heat in Arizona.

At home, I told her that the state director's letters sent out that past spring bore fruit and that I had been offered a job in the lower 48.

"Really, that's great!" she exclaimed. "Where's the job located?"

My response was to tell her how beautiful and mountainous the country was, adding that there would be vast new areas to explore. I was real careful not to mention the absence of trees.

"Wow! That's awesome," she exclaimed, "but where is it?"

I went on to tell her how I could write my own ticket if I could pull this off without a glitch.

She asked again with a hint of impatience, "Where is this job?"

I went on about the need to put together a program for the entire BLM, spelling out how it was a congressional mandate. I emphasized the visibility I would have.

Losing enthusiasm, she finally demanded, "*Where is* this job?"

I winced and told her, "I'll be working on the Mojave Desert." Immediately I received the reaction I expected.

Her memory of Phoenix was altogether too fresh in her mind. "It's hot down there!"

We talked about it long into the night. If I succeeded at this job, we probably would be able to move again in three to five years. Therefore we could look at it as a temporary move. Even so, I really didn't want to leave Alaska any more than Barbi did. We both liked the rough Alaskan culture. Plus, its people seemed to be more accepting of my independence. In view of that, I began arguing against the move a bit. She began to see the distinct advantages to my career and started arguing in favor of such a move. I nearly convinced myself that we should stay, as she was persuading herself that we could probably hold out long enough in California to move to a cooler climate. It was a credit to my bride that she finally saw transferring to California as a positive move. She convinced me to put everything I had into seizing the opportunity.

The following Monday I accepted the job and worked out the details to be there in six weeks. I was twenty-six years old and on the path of a very promising career.

In December, Dad, Mom, Jerry, and Keith traveled to Alaska to spend the holiday with us. This was the third Christmas Barbi and I would spend together. As was becoming our tradition, we cut a black spruce from the dense forest that haunted the fringes of Anchorage. We made a few more ornaments to add to those of the past two Christmases. We still had no lights on our tree, but it was festive to us.

It was both a joyful and sobering time. In the nearly eleven years since my accident, I had come a long way, accomplishing many things.

Lois had struggled for and gained a position as a journeyman pipe insulator working on the Alaska Pipeline Project. She consequently had much to show for herself. Jerry was successfully shoeing horses and working ranches with the goal of raising his own cattle. Keith was in his senior year of high school. I was proud to have my family there in Alaska.

I had left home in Oregon more than five years earlier on a venture to live in Alaska, with little more than a can-do attitude and hope. I now had something to show for it. I hoped that my own personal successes might overshadow my condition, proving I could contribute to society without government assistance. All around, it was also good to celebrate Christmas together. Although we couldn't have known it, it would be the last Christmas our family would ever be together again.

For me personally, it was a send-off for a career I had pursued most of my life. Soon I'd be working outdoors in the field of natural resource management. Barbi and I would be leaving Alaska in less than a month. I was riding high on a dream.

California at that time had a reputation for its concentration of hippies and welfare recipients. This caused eyebrows to rise in a family of self-made conservatives. Teasingly we were ridiculed. "So, you're going to join the hippies, huh?" Despite my success, the ribbing humbled me.

On New Year's Eve, we gathered down at The Pines in Anchorage for a few drinks and some country music. One drink led to another, as we toasted our various successes in life. Since we had much to toast over, we had a lot to drink. With the approach of midnight, we became a little rowdy. The commotion of the dance hall masked our raucous behavior for awhile, so we weren't noticed. Furthermore, the pace of the evening was gradually gaining momentum. Suddenly, someone shouted, "It's midnight!" A round of cheers went through the room, and the band played "Auld Lang Syne." Spontaneously the air filled with a hundred raspy intoxicated voices. All moved along in heartfelt dissonance with the tune. Outside, the cold weather starkly contrasted with the warmth shared by everyone inside.

After that, the music quickened its pace. Others joined us. Raising our drinks with yet another round to bring in the New Year of 1979, someone jumped on the table and started dancing to the music. That's when we became noticeable. As we toasted yet another round to our successes, the bouncer came on the scene, threatening us to settle down or leave. Moreover, he demanded that the dancer get off the table.

At that time, Barbi said she'd celebrated enough and wanted to go home. Mom chimed in, saying the cigarette smoke was getting to her, and the rest of the family decided it was time to head for the barn and bed. Jerry and I, feeling the night was still young, decided to stay on celebrating a while longer. We had met a captain in the Air Force and were indeed still having a great time.

Perhaps an hour after the family left, the three of us walked outside for some fresh air. The temperature felt like well below zero. As the cold night air lashed out at us, we came to our senses, marking the wisdom in heading for home. While we were saying our goodbyes to the captain, two guys emerged from the shadows. Jerry, a few feet away, had started to walk toward the Scout and these guys intercepted him, talking in low voices. I heard Jerry raise his voice and caught his last words, "Why don't you jaybirds just move along." With that, one of the guys whipped something from his pocket and sprayed Jerry in the face. Jerry went down like a moose shot between the ears, as two more guys rushed out of the shadows and jumped the captain.

It really hadn't sunk in yet what happened to Jerry. Foggy from too many drinks, I tried to reason why he went down like he did. Mere seconds passed before the guy with the spray can turned it on me. I reckoning if this took Jerry down, it might not be healthy to catch it in my face. I ducked. It was a second too late. The spray hit my left eye, but my hat took the brunt, as I swung out at the guy. My eye and face suddenly came on fire, but I could still see through my right eye. Two guys had the captain on the ground and were working him over. With the guy holding the spray can momentarily out of sight, I struck a blow to the kidney of one of the two guys on the captain. The guy I hit let out a groan, rolling off to the side, as the captain regained his stand, taking revenge on the other.

Jerry was being worked over by a fourth guy, yet amazingly whenever he could make contact, he held his own while completely blind. Abruptly, someone hit me hard from behind on the blind side of my face. It felt like a hot branding iron struck me, driving the fire deeper into my face. I swung wildly behind me with the armrest of my chair making solid contact on someone I couldn't see, as a possible fifth guy kicked me in the head from a different direction. The captain, now fully recovered, was tying two of the guys into knots. Then mysteriously, the whole gang took flight toward a car in the parking lot to make a getaway. Unfortunately for them, their car wouldn't start.

The whole fight took less than minutes, but the searing pain from the spray made it seem like hours. Fearing the law might show up and cast dispersion on his good character, the captain wished us the best of luck and disappeared. I was uncertain what we'd been sprayed with, but I suspected it was acid. Jerry and I ran into the men's room of the bar, tossing our heads under the faucets to wash off the spray. The cold water relieved the intense pain, but it was still nearly unbearable.

I returned to the bar for help from a guy that I knew casually in a store I frequented on Muldoon Road. I'll call him Ted. He was an evenhanded sort of guy that took to minding his own business. He was quietly visiting with some friends. Seeing that I had been worked over pretty badly, he offered to help find out what we'd been sprayed with. Together we headed back out into the parking lot in hopes of catching the culprits. One of Ted's friends followed, but stayed in the shadows.

The guys who ambushed us had their hood up and were tinkering with their car, still trying to start it. I was sure that we were in for another donnybrook. As Ted spotted them, though, I was startled to see him pull an automatic pistol from under his coat. Dropping down on one knee he pointed the weapon over their heads, hollering at them to freeze. Seeing Ted with a firearm pointing toward them threw cold water on their willingness to fight. They took flight like a pack of coyotes. The guy with the spray can was still holding it in his hand, running as fast as he could across the parking lot.

Again Ted hollered, leveling his weapon on the assailant, "Drop the can or I'll shoot." Apparently the guy had no love affair with what he held in his hand, for he dropped it like a poisonous snake.

Ted picked up the canister and discovered that it was only mace, which relieved us greatly. He then went over to his pickup and emerged with a large baseball bat. Walking to the disabled car, he took out the windshield. Stunned, I almost forgot how bad my face was burning. As he walked toward me, he casually commented, "They won't be driving their car tonight in this cold."

Recoiling, I thanked Ted for his help. He and his buddy went back to join their friends at his table, while I detoured into the men's room to see how Jerry was doing.

He was still trying to subdue the pain in his eyes and face under the cold water. I explained what had happened trying to show him the canister, but he couldn't focus his eyes enough to see it. Again, submerging my face under another faucet helped make the pain tolerable. Totaling our injuries, Jerry's eyes and face were badly swollen and bloody. It was then I caught a look at myself in the mirror. The whole left side of my face was red, puffy, and minced. Everything viewed through my left eye was blurry. Jerry, still blinded by the mace, could barely make it to the Scout.

Warily we headed outside, searching the shadows along the way. I asked Jerry, "What did you *say* to those guys that made them take to the warpath?"

"They wanted to sell us some drugs, and I told those jaybirds to get lost." After a moment, he added, "I guess they didn't like being called jaybirds."

By the time we arrived home, it was more early morning than late night. We were freezing cold, but glad to be home in one piece. The pain eventually began to die down to where we were able to get some sleep. Later that morning, my face still stung, but not anything like the night before. To my dismay, I discovered my hat was permanently stained. It took the brunt of the mace. We didn't get much sympathy from the home front, as people rolled out of bed. Barbi said she knew we were bucking for some kind of trouble. That's why she wanted to go home. The rest of the family stayed quiet, and a few shook their heads.

The winds of time seem to blow clean and fast when it comes to youth, sweeping away troubles with a gust of audacity. Unruly as it was, it did seem to undergird a sense of confidence in my capability. In a day or two, it merely became part of life's history, elapsed into the cloudy waters of shadowed memories, occasionally surfacing to remind me that I was once young and invincible, despite being in a wheelchair.

By January, the ball was in full motion to move to California by the tenth. After the folks left, the crunch of time bore down on us. We had called Barbi's Uncle Clayton and asked if he would be willing to fly up to Anchorage and help us drive down the Alcan Highway. He had driven it many times. His experience and knowledge of the roadhouses along the way would come in handy.

Uncle Clayton arrived about the time the movers finished packing our household goods. We packed some separate items for the drive south. This included a Spartan complement of household items that we anticipated needing during our initial time in California. After everything was moved out, we began camping in our trailer, as we waited for the chilling temperatures to break within the interior continent. The settlement at Watson Lake, Yukon Territory in Canada had been experiencing a cold snap with temperatures dipping down as low as -61° with the wind chill factor around -90°. We could travel at -40° or possibly -50°, but -90° was too cold.

While we waited, a friend named Tom Hardy asked if he could follow us south. In the north, it's often wise to caravan during the winter in the event a vehicle breakdown occurs. At that time, it was even more advisable, since we faced about one thousand five hundred miles of gravel road, and civilization two hundred to four hundred miles apart.

Pleased to have someone to travel with us, we warned him to be ready to leave at a moment's notice. In the meantime, we built a platform in the back of the Scout. The bed of the platform was about four inches below the backrest of the front seat, extending all the way to the tailgate. Upon this we laid several blankets. The sides, top, and back were also lined. Someone could crawl into this 'boot' and sleep while two people sat up front. Our gear was all loaded beneath the platform.

We waited for nearly ten days beyond our scheduled departure date. Even so, the weather was not changing significantly. On the January 9 and 10, the temperature at Watson Lake warmed to -14°, but then plummeted to -48° and began getting colder. The office in California, pressed by the Washington office, was in urgent need for me to start work. BLM management in Washington and the Riverside District Office completely lacked any understanding of the dangers inherent in driving through the extreme cold we were facing. Their only concern was that I get down there and go to work.

It didn't look like the weather was going to break any time soon, and we felt like we were between a rock and a hard spot. Besides, we were getting tired of camping in the trailer. Finally we felt obliged to head south, despite the weather. If our vehicle froze in the interior, we would call and tell them that we were doing our best, but they would just have to be patient.

We traveled an average of four hundred miles a day for the next five days. Average speed was 30 mph due to the ice and snow. The chill factor at 30 mph and -40° is -80°. Traffic on the road was sparse to nonexistent. We didn't see more than four or five vehicles in any given day. Between Tok and Whitehorse, Tom lost control of his car and plowed into a snow bank. Although we lost some time freeing him, nearly tearing the bumper off our Scout, it was fortunate we were there.

Each settlement we drove into seemed to be in a frenzy of activity. Folks claimed that they were suddenly experiencing a warm spell. Even so, the Scout was so cold inside that we were forced to direct the heat full blast through the defrosters. We had no heat to spare for the floor. Bundled in snow boots and parkas inside the vehicle, we were still very cold. Be that as it may, whoever was driving had to keep an ice scrapper close at hand to scrape the inside of the windshield repeatedly. Still, the driver could clear only about a ten-inch area of the windshield.

In those temperatures, the steering system was frozen stiff. Whoever drove needed to begin executing a turn long before reaching a curve in the road. The brakes operated the same way. The pedal pressed down so slowly, that the driver always had to begin breaking long before the need arose. It was almost like conning a ship. More than once, the thought crossed my mind that God was protecting us mile after lonely mile down that highway.

At Watson Lake, we stopped for fuel about 2:00 p.m., as the sun was going down. A light ice fog was in the air, while moisture billowed from any open door like a white cloud and lingered in the air. Every breath a person exhaled was visible. The thermometer at the gas station we pulled into registered -27°. It seemed like the local residents were taking advantage of the warm weather. To the local folks, going from -55° the day before to -27° was a real warm spell. It could have been Christmas Eve with all the pedestrian traffic in town. Some wore light jackets with no hats. We took on a few snacks and fuel, quickly resuming our travel. That day from Whitehorse to Muncho Lake was the longest day we spent on the road.

About 7:00 p.m., we were all pretty jaded. It had been black outside for hours with only headlight beams reflecting off the white frozen roadway. There were no road reflectors to define the edge of the road, making it tiring to drive. The person in the passenger seat either chose to sleep or stare at the soft light reflecting through the icy windshield.

I was driving while visiting with Uncle Clayton in the passenger seat. Barbi was asleep in the boot. The monotone of the wheels on the frozen crystallized roadbed droned beneath us, as we moved along at a top speed of 35 mph. Outside of the Scout, the chill factor was severe. Occasionally I checked for Tom's headlights piercing the darkness behind us.

Rounding a curve, I announced that the lights of a roadhouse appeared near Coal River. Uncle Clayton knew of the place and instructed me to pull off the road and add fuel to the tank. Tom pulled up to a second gas pump. We hadn't seen another person or inhabited building since leaving Watson Lake and were getting mighty tired and hungry. A soft illumination through the roadhouse windows cast the only light outside, as we filled the tanks. The proprietor was surprised to see someone. "It's pretty cold to be traveling, ain't it?" he offered curiously.

"Yes. I have a job in the states, and they're chomping at the bit to have me down there," I replied in a weary tone.

Topping off our tank, he asked, "Is there anything else you need?"

With a drained sigh, I asked, "Is there any chance you might have some supper you would sell us?"

"Nobody's been through here since this afternoon, and we closed up the café hours ago," he regretfully answered. Even in the semi-lighted darkness, I think he could see the hangdog look we must have had on our faces. Thoughtfully he interjected, "Just a moment. I'll ask my wife if she has anything we might offer you." With that, he disappeared into the building. We waited restlessly, wondering if it was wise to spend time standing around when we still had many miles to put between Coal River and Muncho Lake.

After what seemed like a long spell, he popped out of the roadhouse. "Com'on in folks," he said cheerfully.

Inside, the room was warm and inviting. A soft yellow glow radiated from above. I realized for the first time that day how cold I had become. My body was numb all over, and my arms felt like they were moving as stiff as the Scout's steering. Suddenly I was aware of how many clothes I was wearing and began to loosen ties and zippers.

The man's wife appeared from a back room with a warm, pleasant smile. "Take your coats off and set them down over here." She pointed to some benches with hooks on the wall above them. "I can get you some goulash if you don't mind. It's leftovers from the supper our family just ate." We certainly didn't mind one little bit.

"That sounds great!" I said.

My stomach was beginning to think my throat had been cut. She seated us at a small table with a red plaid tablecloth.

"Would you like some coffee?"

Eagerly we answered, "Yes!"

I've traveled across this continent and some in South America, and to this day, that was the best meal I've ever eaten away from home. Perhaps it was the friendly warm atmosphere contrasted with the bleak and bitter cold that lingered like a silent killer stalking us just beyond the door. In any case, we were all refreshed and ready to drive the last leg of the night's journey on to Muncho Lake.

Outside we bundled up against the cold, as we piled into our vehicles. It was the only time during the entire journey I questioned Uncle Clayton's judgment to press on into the dark of the night. The temperatures felt much colder than they had been at Watson Lake earlier that afternoon. Beneath us, the ice screamed its opposition to any movement across it.

Arriving at Muncho Lake, we took lodging in two small one-room log cabins. We went through our routine unloading the vehicles, brought the battery and our crock of sourdough inside, and made straight for the beds. Bone weary from fourteen hours of travel, we crashed. The heaters were running nonstop, but the cabins were barely warm enough to undress and jump in under the blankets.

About four o'clock in the morning, I awoke in a terrible heat. Tossing the covers off, I climbed into my chair and groped for the switch on the heater. The room was stifling hot. After locating the switch, I opened the front door and was hit by what felt like a balmy waft of air.

For a spell, I sat there, gazing into the darkness of the woods. A lone light set on a pole cast a soft glow and long shadows around the area between the cabins where there were a few scattered trees. The surrounding cabins were all dark inside, save one. Outside the air was perfectly still, adding to the silence of the woods.

As I sat there, a young man came out of the lighted cabin nearby and discovered the tire on his vehicle was flat. From my doorway, I softly called out, trying not to awaken Barbi, "Just a minute. I'll give you a hand." Pulling on my pants and mukluks, I went outside with only my long johns covering my upper half. The cabin was still very warm, so I left the door open. Grabbing the handyman jack off the Scout, we quickly changed the tire, and then paused to visit.

Soon Barbi wakened from hearing our voices and came to the door. With a hint of irritation, she crowed, "What in the world are you doing out there this time of the night, and why did you leave the door open!"

"Look," I exclaimed with a note of elation and outstretched arms, "It warmed up during the night."

Barbi was having a hard time sharing my excitement, standing there in her nightgown. She leaned out to look at a thermometer and with an outcry of displeasure proclaimed indignantly, "It's 18°!"

Immediately I shot back, "That's 45° warmer than it was when we stopped here last night!"

Still very tired and not impressed, she responded, "It's still last night! Come to bed!"

The guy thanked me for the help, and I returned to our cabin. Before I crawled back into bed, I cracked the door open about four inches, and then fell into a deep sleep for the first time that trip.

At Fort Nelson, we got out to stretch and buy fuel. Then we discovered the heater motor had burned out and would no longer run. For awhile, we were in a dither over it. Nobody in Fort Nelson had a motor to replace it. Although the weather had warmed up considerably, we still needed it to keep the windshield clear; the ice scraper alone was not adequate. A quarter of an inch of ice had built up on the inside of the windows, except for the small area where we'd been scraping for over a thousand miles. We slowly drove through Fort Nelson and had a terrible time keeping the ice off enough to see. A couple of times, we nearly had an accident. As we drove toward an auto store outside of town, we picked up our speed. It seemed like a miracle happened. The breeze blowing across the engine also blew through the defroster taking the frost with it.

As long as we were moving at a good clip, we could keep a small area of the driver's windshield clear. After we discovered that we didn't need the motor, we kept moving down the highway. Shortly thereafter, we turned south through British Columbia. The ice began to thaw, as we quickly moved into the southern latitudes. The driver's round ice portal expanded also. By the time we arrived in the vicinity of the Peace River, we no longer had to battle ice on the windshield.

There, we spent the night in a small motel on the bank of the river. It is said that anyone who drinks from the Peace River will return one day. That evening on the shore of the Peace River, I gazed to the north. In heartfelt wonder, I pondered how its imprint had changed my life. When I crossed that river I felt that I had left the North, but not forever. I knew one day I'd return. The next day was the fifth day of our journey. We picked up speed, drove to Williams Lake, and spent the night.

In our minds, we had accomplished a great feat, traveling through the North Country in the dead of winter. Once again we had danced on the cutting edge and come out unscathed. We crossed over one thousand five hundred miles of gravel roads paved with ice, covering a total distance of two thousand five hundred miles to Seattle. Several times, we found ourselves all alone, prey to the stalking white reaper that insidiously ravages the hale and hearty to extinguish life. Even so, I believe now as I did then, that the unseen hand of God safeguarded our journey. The extreme cold weather consistently parted before us, so that we never experienced any of the extreme temperatures within the interior that threatened us. I will always be thankful for that.

We arrived in Riverside, California, near the end of January and reported to the office in mukluk boots and parka. Obviously I felt overdressed. They were freezing, however. Envious, someone wondered where they could get some warm winter clothing like I was wearing. Someone suggested that perhaps I had brought the northern cold down with me.

That winter in Southern California was one of the coldest on record with high moisture and flooding recorded throughout the region. If only I could have shown them the face of real cold, I surely would have received some droll satisfaction for being forced to drive through it.

EPILOGUE

Relentlessly, like the wheels of my chair, time rolled into another year. Behind us, Alaska faded into memories. I realized more than ten years had now passed since that tragic night in Oregon's high Cascades. Despite the many adjustments I'd made, my body continued to ambush me. Mentally I still reeled from the loss of my legs. An inner void lingered constantly, threatening to consume me.

Naturalism brought me closer to reasoning through my suffering, yet to fully grasp what it meant to endure this as a man eluded me. Somehow I sensed that to be human involved more than nature's brutal forces of struggle and survival of the fittest. But with little else to cling to, I tenaciously held onto my own beliefs.

Benefits and risks lay ahead in unforeseen challenges. The isolation and fierce heat of the Mojave Desert brought trials that defy imagination. Later, working alone in the remote Rocky Mountains brought new perils. Would I dare accept the land's harsh challenges? To answer that question, I needed to find a source of unfailing courage. While searching for that, I found myself faced with two basic questions: How badly did I want this courage, and did I dare pay the price to receive it? I struggled to gauge what kind of inner strength I might need to wage everything in search of ultimate answers.

Intuitively I felt that the source of these answers impinged on one question that always had haunted me: *Why did I live through that fateful night in June of 1968?* Could it have been a miracle or simply a series of chance random events that brought me to this point? Did the natural laws *really* act as mindless forces on all life or did a watchful guiding force orchestrate all of nature?

Life blitzed forward in a series of contradictions. I found myself torn between hope and despair, courage and doubt, freedom and bondage. Insidious pressure from these contradictions often overwhelmed me.

Outwardly I raged against those who saw me only as a wheelchair. Frankly, anger only screened my real feelings. Grief at the vortex of that inner, howling abyss always left me feeling helpless. I couldn't walk! A mean-spirited demeanor hardened around me, protecting my vulnerable areas from the people I merely viewed as competition in nature's food chain.

Eventually, however, satisfying answers slowly emerged. The passing years brought many changes. Barbi and I had children of our own. An unimaginable outdoor job career developed within the BLM. After the Mojave Desert, I worked throughout the Rocky Mountains in rough and remote country to get gas and electric power to the rest of the United States. By the time I reached forty, I had driven thousands of miles across rugged country in four-wheel-drive pickup trucks. Furthermore, my job allowed me to travel hundreds of miles on snowmobiles while working the back country in subzero winter conditions. Helping to route one of the first snowmobile trails across the Continental Divide in Wyoming became one of many highlights of my job. It opened new avenues to explore the mountains I came to love.

In 1983, I became a Christian. Consequently I began to assess my situation in a different light. I saw that my life had purpose. As I accepted the truth of why I survived that accident in 1968, doors of success opened. Along the way, inner peace entered my life, filling that old void. Later, an understanding of these things became essential to surviving heart-wrenching personal tragedies. Future events would put to the fire everything I held dear.

Perhaps you can identify with many of the struggles described in the pages of this book. Insurmountable difficulties can often paralyze our minds, preventing us from reaching for life's full potential. If you can identify with these words, I dare you to travel with me, as I continue my journey of discovery and uncover a special hope that allows me to look beyond myself. In the process, I discover new strength to strive for life's blessings and ways to share them with others.

Coming soon...

Vanquishing the Void

A Paraplegic Discovers New Life and Purpose
Beyond the Confines of His Wheelchair

By David E. Harper